The Figure Going Imaginary

The Figure Going Imaginary

LIFE DRAWING   POETRY   THE CADAVER LAB

a year in pieces

Marianne Boruch

COPPER CANYON PRESS

PORT TOWNSEND, WASHINGTON

Cover art by Marianne Boruch.
All drawings included in the book are by Marianne Boruch.

Copper Canyon Press is in residence at Fort Worden State Park
in Port Townsend, Washington, under the auspices of Centrum.
Centrum is a gathering place for artists and creative thinkers from
around the world, students of all ages and backgrounds, and
audiences seeking extraordinary cultural enrichment.

LIBRARY OF CONGRESS CATALOGING-IN-PUBLICATION DATA
Names: Boruch, Marianne, 1950– author.
Title: The figure going imaginary : life drawing, poetry, the cadaver lab:
    a year in pieces / Marianne Boruch.
Description: Port Townsend, Washington : Copper Canyon Press, 2025. |
    Summary: "A memoir of journal notes, early drafts of poems, and short
    meditations by Marianne Boruch"— Provided by publisher.
Identifiers: LCCN 2024010376 (print) | LCCN 2024010377 (ebook) |
    ISBN 9781556596940 (paperback) | ISBN 9781619323025 (epub)
Subjects: LCGFT: Essays. | Poetry.
Classification: LCC PS3552.O75645 F54 2025 (print) |
    LCC PS3552.O75645 (ebook) | DDC 811/.54—dc23/eng/20240311
LC record available at https://lccn.loc.gov/2024010376
LC ebook record available at https://lccn.loc.gov/2024010377

9 8 7 6 5 4 3 2 FIRST PRINTING

COPPER CANYON PRESS
Post Office Box 271
Port Townsend, Washington 98368
www.coppercanyonpress.org

for my grandmother Aileen Jones Taylor (1883–1970), who would have been astounded and unnerved as I was by this very notion

for my brother, Michael, who was braver than either of us: "Sometimes everywhere I look, I see"

. . . clay and straw over an iron and wickerwork frame.
Arm = bundles of sticks tied, string circling it, clay on that.
Wings of basic wood rods, straw woven.

From the museum label—a so-called tombstone—
for a 1673 study for Gian Lorenzo Bernini's sculpture
Angelo di destra.

The Vatican Museums, Rome.

(*Angel bent, lips parted . . .*)

Contents

The Figure Going Imaginary

I Will Explain Why in a Moment

Here's that moment: some books get strange even before they're imagined. This one, a precursor in retrospect, seemed to gather itself like an assemblage of tea leaves gradually darkening the water in a blue pot. It's a gaggle of "research" on repeat repeat repeat of evolving form and content, words and phrases coming up again and again as in dream; an architectural attempt because I grew envious of ants, how they expertly—anciently—build ant hills, or of termites, how they work on their life-sustaining towers in the desolate Outback of Australia while humans can get lost and die from heat and dehydration there.

I lay that out right now, a warning.

In truth, this is a book of ammo *toward* poems. A fate not clear at all when these notes came to be, moment after moment observed in lab and studio and put to paper. It is, after all, not the finished product to be locked away with a key. This is the long haul *behind* certain poems, the wanna-be flying buttress for a book coming later and, as such, an example and perhaps of use to others who make poems or read them or ignore them completely and are just curious about what goes on in a so-called cadaver lab of a medical school. Or in a life-drawing class where people stop time to invent on paper what they think or dream they see in the human figure in a rare moment, many moments, of stillness. Or to note in whatever jots and serious squibs what continues to lie in wait behind glass in museums of great cities and kept safe, ongoing bits of bone and history, elixirs no one believes in anymore, grim stories of death and rescue, outrageous evidence of surgery, healing know-how (or know-nothing) from prehistory through the Black Plague, inching toward us via crutch and childbirth and wars and centuries and both robust and toxic harvests—to what? Now? To our recent plagued months possibly turning into years?

It's not always the coins dropped one by one. But time and what it hoards do come to us in pieces.

Because we can't see everything at once, I slow it up here, this instance of hardcore backdrop to the making of poems published later. Or I am simply tracing a habit familiar and weird, learning to look at two things at once. In this case, poetry and medicine, imagination and fact. So I sometimes thought.

The thing is—

A week or so before Thanksgiving, 2007, I walked to an unfamiliar part of Purdue University, where I had taught in the English Department since 1987. I was looking for the anatomist James Walker who ran the cadaver lab, the Gross Human Anatomy class at the Indiana University Medical School, its regional branch secreted away in the basement of Purdue's vet school then, Professor Walker's office too, both bits of the world hard to find for a liberal arts sort like me, set in her ways on the other side of that particular planet, if a university can be called that.

Finally a door, and an elevator down. "I'm a poet from the English Department," I told him after the usual introductory pleasantries, then launched straightaway into the reason I had turned up that late fall afternoon. As a proper alien in that territory of medicine and repair and hope, I spoke with only one of my heads and lowered my antennae.

"There's this Faculty Fellowship in the Study of a Second Discipline, run by the provost's office," I said. "I want to apply. You know, to participate in or simply audit your Gross Human Anatomy course in whatever way you might allow next year. Fall semester, I mean." He stared, puzzled but expectant. Surely there was more to this. "And so I'm wondering if you might consider that."

My words rushed the air between us. I could feel his quiet computing my unorthodox request. Perhaps he was picturing it with genuine dismay: a poet in his cadaver lab between those steel tables under the glare of the overhead lights—a *what-in-the-world?* And really, to do *what?* Write poems? Would I be wandering about the lab in pince-nez and beret (I do wear an old beret, walked in with it on probably), wielding a pen and notebook, underfoot and annoying, uttering rattled-to-the-core crazy proclamations? Professor Walker—Jim—seemed dubious, only politely intrigued, then . . .

"Great!" he beamed at last with what would turn out to be his characteristic cheer. "Okay! Sure!" And in a perfectly offhand upbeat way: "How about a visit right now? Lab is over for the day but it's November—we just unwrapped the heads."

Yes, he did say *heads.* A small new horror welled up in me: *we just unwrapped the* . . .

"Uh, well, not yet," I heard myself blurt out. "I mean, if this provost's fellowship comes through, I'll want the experience *as it happens,* start to finish, next fall." *If* I do it, I really meant then—and for weeks and months through winter unto spring and summer, even after I was given the go-ahead to start the whole alarming business in late August 2008.

Truth is I wanted to launch new poems and an essay or two that would surprise, even upend me. Considering academia's usual straight-ahead insistence on focus in *one* area only and no digressions off one's vita that might mark one as a dilettante and weaken the reputation of both scholar and supporting institution, the crucial requirement of that fellowship was refreshingly unthinkable. It meant *time off* in the purest sense—from teaching, from one's usual pursuits—offering Purdue faculty the chance to work in an area having virtually nothing to do with what they'd been doing forever. New territory was the rule and expectation. Expansion, curiosity, breaking age-old habits for fresh connections—that was the thrilling part. Even the thought felt revolutionary, closer to dream. And besides, I am no scholar, merely a poet.

As it happens, I did get lucky—a dark luck, it turned out. I was awarded the fellowship, given a place to observe in the human dissection lab, and, on alternate days—a lovely foil, matter to those antimatter hours in the med school—I'd be a student across campus in a life-drawing class taught by the artist Grace Benedict of Art & Design, who also kindly welcomed me. But in that particular space, in the studio, I *had* to draw—my future teacher would not budge on that. So no, I wouldn't be allowed just to sit there and work on poems while my classmates drew and redrew and set themselves to the ancient task of learning to see.

Clearly, what a bizarre autumn ahead, staring at and into bodies, living and dead.

Careful what you wish for, etc., etc. . . . is the common way to register *be warned.* At times, as my anxiety grew, that old comedy line rubbed it in too. *Well, here's another fine mess you've gotten me into,* Hardy says to Laurel, a phrase that echoes another beloved complaint from that era: *What we have here is a fine kettle of fish!*

I told myself there *was* purpose to this kettle, these fish, and reason enough. Poets exhaust the past, years autodigging into memory for poems. Over four decades *in,* I'd been there, done that, seven poetry collections' worth at that point, orbiting and unearthing

    Childhood, check—

    Young adulthood, check—

    Marriage, check—

    Motherhood, check—

    Glad and deeply unglad moments, check—

    Definitely love of all sorts, check—

    Death and its many guises. Check of course, of course—

    All of the above, the usual suspects for poets.

Which is to say it wasn't exactly *so what,* more a big blank *now what?* It seemed simple and, in spirit, matching the faculty fellowship exactly: find some unimaginable situation that requires a measure of risk, if not madness, and promise full, however troubled, attention to it. I figured it would be near enough to my usual practice, my begging-bowl theory of how to write. Do nothing willful, cook up no agenda. Instead go empty, work with whatever drops in.

But this was a hell of a drop to invite into that bowl.

So I worried. Was the whole business too prescribed now? I'd asked for—had been given and now assigned—a job description, something specific to do, however unnerving that dreaming off would be. I'd need to stay alert in that cadaver lab for a semester, take notes, be jolted and amazed. And in Life Drawing? Just be there, pencil in hand to make my awful honest-to-Zeus drawings in the studio those months. Maybe my beginner's mind would welcome it all.

As in: what to make of such strangeness?

As in: have patience.

But what would I end up writing, if anything? Here's the mantra I already knew by heart:

> poems are lyric devices
>
> poems are lyric devices
>
> poems are lyric devices . . .
>
> often dangerous implosions.

Thus that fall I got duly outfitted by the med school—a hand-me-down white lab coat and blue scrubs, a locker for my civilian clothes when I was in the lab, a built-in combination lock with numbers and letters to commit to memory. The students' books became my books. Frank Netter's *Atlas of Human Anatomy,* and the thousand-pound textbook Jim Walker was using, *Clinically Oriented Anatomy* by Moore and Dalley. Plus the unnerving, predictably gruesome but standard nearly two centuries now, maybe the most unsettling how-to manual ever written—*The Dissector*—close to what poet John Keats used in the reeking shambles of his cadaver lab at Guy's Hospital in London in the early 19th century, its matter-of-fact human horrifics of dissection calmly rendered step by step in those pages that probably guided the good doctor-poet William Carlos Williams too, en route to his *contagious* hospital. Because there's history and practice behind the body, the study of medicine as a compelling launch into poetry. It's all eyes in dissection lab, danger on four sides. I would weapon-up with that most primal tool, a scalpel. The *immediate* is everything in that bone-white room. But so ancient too; every detail of the body goes back to prehistory. Everything would be endlessly larger than my tiny thoughts of it.

In my other life that semester, in Life Drawing class, I acquired tools equally archaic: charcoal, brush and black ink, pencils—every darkening sort—and colorful chalks, plus the shrewd patient eraser, frenemy to each mark I laid down. I bought a huge black satchel for all this ammo, tablets of newsprint, and decent paper.

My drill became: Mon, Wed, Fri, 8 a.m. to 1 p.m., for the cadavers themselves; 12 hours a week for the old and the dead, the four lost ones who floated months in evil chemicals to get there, laid out on four gleaming metal tables. Tue and Thu, three hours each of those days, for my walk into studio, going blank before whatever model, mainly the beautiful young, their faces blank too but held in actual living time unlike the four beyond time in their permanent stillness several buildings away.

In Life Drawing though, you could hear it: charcoal to paper, a netherworld sound, all rush and hesitation of the doing itself, a secret, a *how-does-it-know?* I mean the hand at it, at it— concentration the sweet thing.

Keep looking, my teacher said when I felt sure my drawing finished.

That was a while ago now. But I can't stop relearning what I learned, the same way I couldn't get the lab smell completely out of my hair those months, or what it felt like in drawing class, bringing living fellow humans to paper. Of course, my old, most quiet of compatriots laid out in that cold room for dissection, they came to life too.

Done, you're undone. And what I write even now so often bears the touch of that double Janus-faced experience, my looking forward or back, then two approaches, two contexts to the body as backdrop, as metaphor or dream, as fact—a darkness, an inevitable reach through time and place, ancient and modern, whatever such layering may mean. In both, the body floats regardless.

As for method, it changed for me *as a writer* that curious semester. Time at home at my desk I've called my *hospital rounds* ever since, each early morning's hovering over the poems or whatever essay I'm working on. I check in, visit with my drafts, whatever their state of undress. Pencil in hand as if at a sketchbook, I look, keep looking weeks, months, even years as images shift down through revision into an unsettling final *other* with, then without me.

The solace of habit is straight up, reliably weird. World we don't think of, have no words for. Then there *are* words. Hospital rounds. A tentative first sketch. It's a method vastly deepened—one I also have passed on to students—through my experience in the cadaver lab and in the life-drawing studio that fall, 2008.

Throughout everything, I kept two journals: a pocket-size one to slap-dash images and observations in both places, and the more stable, larger notebook with a hard cover, to record and reconsider, each late afternoon after those classes, into evening.

I bring into this book entries gathered in the UK too, because my faculty fellowship included visits to revered surgical museums in London and Edinburgh. And later, in spring, in Italy, and thanks to another award, I recorded in a small ledger what I saw and thought in

Bellagio. It was there at the Rockefeller Foundation's 13th-century villa that I wrote the first draft of what would be the title poem of my eighth collection, *Cadaver, Speak,* continuing that work for a couple of weeks as a visiting artist at the American Academy in Rome. Many of those notes made their way here too.

But honestly, my day-by-day that fall in the lab and the studio, bringing me so close to the hard mysteries of the body so thoroughly beyond my commonplace, and the time in the UK and Italy—I need to refocus now. Not that it *changed* me, because that would leave it back there. It *keeps* changing me. At the very least, it has opened and keeps opening the experience of others. Like I can't help imagining Keats writing out of what terrible things he must have seen, those months of medical training at Guy's Hospital, the place where even

> ... youth grows pale, and spectre-thin, and dies;
> Where but to think is to be full of sorrow.

Or so his poems translated that world for him and left it behind for us.

Some time after we actually did unwrap the heads, those faces shrouded in wet towels until November in Jim Walker's dissection lab a year after our first meeting and my awkward request, I stood watching as one of the students hacked away at the neck of the oldest cadaver, my favorite and always profoundly moving to me. How small she was, and those watery blue eyes. The student sawed and strained; she worked hard on that cadaver. The truth is the head doesn't want to leave the body. One of the other students—the most endearing of those in the class, I thought—turned to me.

"You know, sometimes I wonder what all this looks like, to someone from the outside," the young man said. "I mean it's so ..."

I could see my own dark wonder in his face—not a mirror, more like I really could finish his sentence because we'd been there together those past five months tracing back thousands of years of human history in the body itself.

"This is one of those times," he told me, then trailed off because we all stopped talking. It was only the bitten-off teeth of the saw on bone to hear then, the raw ache of that rhythm taking us down to the quick.

Thus this book: my original record of *one of those times* again and again, page after page for five months. And then the putting together over those months that followed an honest-to-god collection of poems, a wayward urgent act of imagination. For the first time in my life I kept a daily journal in that year of making, a way to speak at the *moment of* and later to remember while honoring the vast gobsmacked quiet involved.

It turned out there *were* poems to come from this double experience. And new moves in the mysterious day-to-day process of *making* itself. This book is behind all that. It is the gritty source. I had to write everything down in the plein air of those moments before what I saw got lost. As virtually everything is lost. But there remained the slow climb into poetry, our oldest, most revered literary genre.

Because there is more than silence and tragedy in the world.

I

Shards

little whys and what-ifs—

—Toward some maybe future book: A straight progression off what happened. Elaboration of the journal. This journal. Prose. Or prose and poetry, when poems suit. One long *whoosh.* The usual suspect as speaker—me me me. Or partly that, or none of that, the voices of others taking over.

—Maybe the 100-year-old speaks. Or one of the med students. Or the young artist in drawing class who knows very little English, who put his hands on each side of his face and whispered *Munch* when he saw my terrible self-portrait.

—Look, think, make a mark, she said.

—Identify, appreciate, move on, he said.

—*The Dissector.* Or Keats's *London Dissector,* 1817.

—All those lost unto lost, don't look. Then you do look . . .

—How does Keats come back? Does he? Should he?

—Kinds of drawing like a dazzle of zebras: gesture, blind contour, straight lines only, curves only; x-ray to skeleton, pen and ink, charcoal; the addictive move to color, the awful self-portrait.

—Do artists' notebooks count here? Leonardo's drawings? Michelangelo's? Verbatim what they say? Or: can I get the figures in the drawings to speak? Especially those unfinished, impartial, abandoned on paper by accident or design, in progress forever then, lying there, emergent, about to . . .

—A book done as entries. As second thoughts. As letters home (cadavers from the netherworld, the foreign student in drawing class, Samar disappeared to her pilgrimage to Mecca, all leaving their mark on the page).

—My mother's body in the hospital. Her barely-in-it. My grandmother losing language. My friend June's shrinking memory, 85 years old, only a small *what-just-happened*—three hours' worth perhaps—orbits her pointing to the moon: is that the moon?

—Which is worse? Losing memory or losing language? Are these even separate?

—(*Write* it!) says Elizabeth Bishop. Everything that *means* in a parenthesis.

—The small vial of ear stirrups in the cadaver lab. The plastic tub of spinal cords. Four brains floating in their white buckets across the white room. Listen.

—What is it, that awful scent afterward? En route to my car or going up the stairs.

—One of the med students whose name is *All of Them* as we women change into scrubs in the girl's john says: Oh my god. I'm at a party. And suddenly I smell *cadaver* on me!

—The cadavers' faces, finally unshrouded. Words toward *stunned* (I'm stunned), *beautiful* (they're beautiful), as if the finest charcoal pencil has done its work, their eyes closed or not. Mouths simply made by line, or one is open, calling out her final silent middle of the night.

—What is it to see *gesture,* as if one might see and freeze those standing around a swimming pool or actually in water. Or at Walmart or Pay Less, the deep privacy of each shopper—then just the street outside, some guy walking down that street?

—Of course a new x-ray vision kicks in deeper than skin to bone and vessel and nerve, the darkest dark, its pulse.

—Draw that, I dare you.

—Keep connecting those images, those figures somehow, says my drawing teacher. Do something with the background.

—The quietude of each model in Life Drawing. We take turns when one doesn't show. Me—my turn on the platform—I sink into my baggy sweater. I close my eyes, fending off their eyes.

—In the Elgin Marbles at the British Museum, *their* blank white unseeing eyes. Time has worn off the garish colors the Greeks put there. What colors? Like DayGlo, the docent told me. Terrible colors, she said briskly. Such bad taste. She shook her head.

—My mother near death never wanting to open her eyes in the hospital. Her pretending to sleep—I knew that. Her pretending *no, not here at all.* Outside, all that scaffolding, men fixing something.

—The long underground passage to get to the cadaver lab each Monday, Wednesday, Friday. *These are the catacombs.* But it's just a basement, abandoned file cabinets, broken chairs. *I'm entering the netherworld,* I think and thought at least three weeks in. Then I am rushing past it all. Simply on time. Or I'm late. The elevator door opens to a hallway to get through.

—The chain-mail veil that begins at the base of the ribs, drops down, unsecured at the pelvis, its glistening golden bits of fat, the dizzy wiry turns of ... *what,* for what?

—Think *tabernacle*. Thinking: this is where the Catholics, the Jews got their big idea. The Holy of Holies to protect all transformation, itself a transformation.

—First crucial metaphor is *about* metaphor: the colon, the swirling intestines that change everything into something else. That *take*. Then throw the rest away.

—In Edinburgh, the surgical museum: a musket ball from Waterloo still embedded in the femur. We see the skull sliced not quite through by a saber, jagged cuts in the bony surface, the invisible ink of rage and fear down there.

—How Sherlock Holmes solved those crimes: you diagnose like a doctor obsessed, who thinks of nothing else, who makes the leap, 2 and 2 equals . . . 5!

—Conan Doyle not quite or ever that doctor, though his teacher, Joseph Bell, in Edinburgh, yes.

—The wiring of the body, nerves off the spinal cord, those knobs of vertebrae. But its dot to dot seems suspect, a city built upon city, the old house badly rewired though mainly it works.

—*O what a piece of work is man . . .* Does that praise or question? More amazing: that these jerry-built circuits spark at all.

—Before this, in utero, it's the gut tube, the cardiac tube, their gradual vast and intricate complications to come. We all start—*female*! Only then we grow specific.

—The stillness of the cadaver not like the stillness of the model in drawing class who longs to move her leg, her arm. For whom future is immediate and mundane: oh my god, tell me how many minutes to the 10-minute break.

—Against the usual, ponderous Latinate words for this bony-framed small valley in the body, give me a plain name to love: the hand's *anatomical snuffbox* between thumb and forefinger. Yes!

—Then the empty spaces buried as we lie down and sleep each night, reservoirs to catch and hold until upright again all the excess fluids. Someone found these, assumed they owned them. Plus the skull's interior, its craters and peaks as if the anatomists climbed through the headscape, claimed them for the record books. *Pouch of Morrison,* etc., etc.

—Little junior where one doubled down: Meckel's cave. *O little named-after-me . . .*

II

THE BODY FLOATS REGARDLESS

—notes of origin

8/18   Cadaver Lab

I see soaked tube socks on the cadavers' feet and hands.
Your first patients, says the teacher.
Keep spraying them down with alcohol, fabric softener, water.
Keep them damp.
Take care of your cadaver, he said.

We start a week earlier than the rest of campus, go at the skin then work inward. *Surface anatomy* by feel, so we *palpate.* Where muscles attach to bones = kennings. I love that—*kennings*—Old English for phrases that define wildly by metaphor to bring unlikely worlds together. Like *Beowulf*'s "raven-harvest" equals "corpse."

And bones *articulate.*

On a far wall, an old photograph: wooden tables, cadavers there, medical students in white smocks like those worn in art studios over a century ago. In black script below: "University of Pennsylvania, 1909." And above: "The Lord giveth, the Lord taketh away." The young men look resigned, staring into the camera, which must be five feet off the ground on a long-legged tripod we don't see, a black shroud trailing behind where the photographer hides.

The *anatomical position* means face up, palms open on the table as if the body descended there from god knows where, fell quietly back to earth like a leaf from a great height. Earlier, before we slipped into scrubs and lab coats, a first-day survey: "How would you assess your general

knowledge of human anatomy?" Around me everyone was writing.
Then it was: "Apply what you know."

Like, can you trace a drop of blood through the heart? our teacher Jim
Walker asked.

Translation: Can I trace a drop of blood through a poem?

8/20   *Cadaver Lab*

Deep back. Cranial nerves, their own creatures, part of the brain vs.
spinal accessory nerve, C1 down. A first real lecture. The overhead light
projects the neck muscles and nerves, the spinal cord over Jim Walker's
face. The real and the surreal, another kind of kenning.

> —Most superficial muscles: splenius muscles (*splenius* means
> "bandage").
> —Local spinal nerves innervate the deep back muscles, thus
> posture.
> —Deepest muscles: in grooves on either side of the spinal column.
> —Kyphosis: humpback.
> —Lordosis: swayback.
> —Scoliosis, a sign: more a twisting of the spine observed when the
> patient bends over.
> —Its curve changes as a person ages (fetus to newborn to old age,
> all of it a stick-with-it-for-decades toward the long lean forward,
> crooked as the staff that shepherds sometimes held.)
> —Spinal discs: Nucleus in the jellylike interior. Dehydrates with
> age, grows thinner.
> —CSF: cerebrospinal fluid—glistening stuff, clear as gin.

A brief visit by an orthopedic doc, the *back* man, the neurosurgeon.
An aside from him: old people bend over to lessen pain by opening
the space between encrusted vertebrae where nerves run and could get

cramped, getting pinched. So my forward-leaning grandmother comes back from the dead.

Afterthought: that doctor's story of those pinched nerves, stress, until the giant brain tumor found. The 20-year-old was sweet, smiling, didn't quite know what to do with his hands. We heard the whole saga. The tumor's discovery, its removal.

So much water in the brain, David told me this afternoon, home early from the VA. Its ponds grow to lakes, whole oceans as we age and the brain loses function.

Some advice for the dissections that follow: to test—pull on the look-alike arteries and nerves. Nerves don't break. Arteries do. Veins are thin walled and appear dark red.

8/22   *Cadaver Lab*

The cadavers at first glance: bog people—if I look hard enough—brought out of ancient waters minus the rope around their waists or their necks, the villagers' rage still in their ears.

The four *old* cadavers; one even made it to 100. The youngster is 74. Two men, two women, gender marked instantly by the trademark appendages and openings. Also the traditional Greek symbols for male, for female on tags at the base of each table underscore that—as if we needed an arrow jetting up toward the right or a cross straight down off a circle to alert us. Then we turn them. Because? The back, our teacher, Jim Walker, tells me, we start with that, the most impersonal part of the body. Less disturbing to the students, he says.

The cadavers' heads, wrapped in damp white towels. The 100-year-old, such a small skull; even under the wrapping, that's clear. I lower my hand and rest it there. And remember my grandmother sleeping. If the soul who left this body came back, under our flashing knives and forceps . . .

I will my warmth to reach her, not to thank, just to coexist. To welcome her—but who am I to do that, still in this world with this scent, this *smell.* Slowly, it sickens. Like mothballs but worse. Because it gains. By the end of the session—four hours or so—people are tearing up against it. Jim Walker warns us about contact lenses.

One cadaver has very little fat, *sub-cu* they call it as we cut into his back. The thickest skin imaginable on that guy. Skin and muscle and fascia. He's huge, tall, and thick—seemingly all muscle though.

Samar Khirallah, an MD trained in Damascus, is here to assist Jim Walker. She wears a headscarf, is meticulous, quietly elegant. And wry at times, half laughing at jokes though altogether earnest. The students love her. Do you think he was an athlete? I ask.

We'd need to see the muscles more fully to decide that, she sensibly says.

Why is fat so yellow? I ask. No one knows. And why do we have it at all?

Heat, padding! one young woman sings out.

Energy, David tells me later. So much of it, all to be scraped away as we dissect.

Want to try? I'm asked at one of the tables. So I get my first small chance, pulling up with tweezers (*forceps* now) and a *sharp* (formerly *knife*). There are *probes* too. And common paper towels at the ready. A vegetarian, I haven't removed fat from chicken for years, but it all floods back. Here I am instructed into what surely is obvious:

    1) You carefully pull up with the forceps and

    2) Cut to the quick with the sharp.

All fat goes into a bucket at the foot of the table, the body's trapezius and the latissimus dorsi gradually revealed, beautiful and pink even in a person this old. Meanwhile the fascia is sticky and clear and everywhere. Jim tells me it envelops every muscle.

Like Saran Wrap, I say brightly.

Sure, he says, like that.

Someone isolates the cranial nerve. *Eureka!* And we all rush over to see it. "The accessory nerve." Other nerves are similar but smaller, thin white wires. We see blue blood vessels embedded in the muscle wall. Then the rhomboideus, major, minor, under the trapezius. But the nerve, maybe the dorsal scapular.

Suddenly, from one of the students: Hey, Doc Walker, can you still eat jerky? And my own stupid joke over the big guy: Gee, we can say anything we want about him. He's really thick-skinned!

No one laughs. Sorry, I say, dumb joke.

I thought it was funny, one young man says kindly.

My gloves are purple. Medium. I'm told to put my name on a whole box of them.

Is this what you expected? Jim asks me.

No idea what to expect, I say.

Could he see my amazement?

Just wait, he tells me.

At an English Department party this evening, a colleague corners me: his mother broke her neck but is fine, is recovering well. Where? I ask as if I know something. The atlas?

When he says the first bone under the head, I see it, my x-ray vision starting to kick in, and abruptly recallable.

Yeah, that's the one, I say, before the guy wanders off for another drink.

C1. But the axis—C2, the real workhorse—goes second. Still, in story and myth, it's Atlas who holds the whole heavy planet on his shoulders.

Odd that people are beginning to tell me such things. As if I am a conduit now, one world to another.

8/25 *Cadaver Lab*

It's the human spinal cord today. Thick. Whitish. In one case veined, those pathways, yes, dark red and circling up slowly. In the lumbar region, where Walker told us to cut the spinal column, the bony vertebra. Its wing nuts, I'd say. Its "processes," they are (weirdly) called.

One group uses a small, handheld circular saw, down on one side of the column, then the other. They give me a turn with that. Another group I watch intently uses hammers and—was it a wedge?

You guys are the traditionalists, I say to the tall English-major-turned-medical-student from Arizona. Not the electric saw? I notice that's what the others use.

Uncivilized, he tells me.

All this so unlike the cool, clean, totally tidy pictures in Frank Netter's *Atlas of Human Anatomy*. But here in this white room, the way cadavers really are, it *is* a *Where's Waldo?* shambles, this carving up the human body after the fact. It really does resemble the poor turkey the day after Thanksgiving, a cheap cliché often pointed out.

Today we're set to the task. Find this arrangement of muscle, a certain triangle of them, that length of spinal cord, this whatever. The body, rich with its interlocking layers, is overwhelming and confusing, this telling *what* from *what,* all the buildup with fascia and fat as mortar. And Netter's carefully drawn depiction? I think of Peterson's bird guides, the drawing there, its decoy-like qualities, main bits exaggerated in those feathered creatures, nesting or caught in the dramatic movement of flight.

These bodies rest now in ways they never did, graciously taking every knife blade, probe, hand slam of wedge and hammer, the teeth of the buzzing saw. Complicated. Eccentric but universal. All the while the Netter and *The Dissector* open, nonchalant on the table or bookstand nearby, pages laid out to show the ideal world of the body.

No, this is *not* that easy, not a cinch. But so beautiful and deep-down secret, stranger and messier.

The spinal cord itself! One group further isolates it, deep in the body. Under light, first time in 90 years. There is a call, great excitement. And we all move over to that table where the students are beaming. All this information, the hands-on feel for it too much for a moment. *I am looking at the spinal cord,* I keep thinking.

Then today, a rarity. One other observer turns up: she and I are told we can look at a fully dissected body from the summer. So we give it a shot on the other side of the room, raising the silver lid like waiters revealing the prized dish in a fancy restaurant. Really, what to call it? Its container? Its lab coffin? I don't know the names of things. We turn back the plastic, the sheet soaked in formaldehyde, the odor even stronger.

The organs—heart, liver, lungs—are in a clear bag atop the body, but we lift the ribs' curvature and see the colon's twisting ropes below.

It's too much, all at once. I want it bit by bit as we dissect in the weeks ahead. The other observer stays on to stare it all down further. She's only here for a day, after all. Minutes later, she signals me from across the room, and together we wrap the body, give it back its plastic shroud and sheet, pull the shiny lid down.

Back, Dear One—whoever you are—to your dark.

8/26   *Life Drawing*

The model is huge and scarred and unashamed. She's older, on oxygen. Her body *knows* things. Has been through the wringer, my mother would have said. The other students and I bear down hard on the paper, superimposing one drawing on the next and the next, a *gesture* drawing. It's like we're making a flip book—but on one page!—an animation as she lies so still.

All these tools to find: pencil, charcoal, paper, ink, brush. What's the relation between eye and hand?

No music, our teacher, Grace Benedict, insists at the onset, laying down the rules. And students remove their earbuds.

> 1) We work hard, she says, but expression doesn't mean "anything goes." One *learns* to be creative.
>
> 2) She says: There are no edges until you get there.
>
> 3) Respond to the heaviest part of the figure first, she says. Density is in the form. (Why do I keep hearing *destiny*?)

I bring home my drawings on those giant sheets of rag paper to show David. He's good to them, thrilled really, like the mom raving over her nine-year-old's start-and-stop screeching violin.

8/27   *Cadaver Lab*

The deltoid, the triceps.

The smell is getting to me. Just opening my locker-o-scrubs-and-lab-coat hits me hard. And then walking again into lab, the bodies quiet as ever, the backs open now, flaked and probed, dug into, cut, sawed, the heads still wrapped. The students go to work on the shoulder, cutting back the deltoid, off the trapezius, off the rhombi, clearing the scapula, that triangular bone. Hard work at hand. To isolate certain muscles, quadrangles and triangles where they dome together, where they frame. Beneath lie blood vessels—veins, arteries—and nerves to isolate.

The men have huge deltoids, especially the huge no-fat guy. I point that out to one group, and ask "Is that a sexist remark?" One woman thinks so. But in this small sample, the difference is stark, even in the thinner-skinned guy, the scrawny one. Both men, their shoulders are larger, more defined.

I'm a fifth wheel here, not knowing exactly what to do, wandering from table to table, trying not to take up too much space. I stare at the gradually dismantled bodies, at how diligent these students—kids to me really—are working their flashing knives and probes and forceps and blotting paper towels as the preserving fluid pools up in the body's depths and begins to seep. No one offers me a turn at the tools this time.

I chat with Jim Walker—my mother-in-law's bad arm just like the picture in his lecture slide this morning, and my own broken collarbone—shoulder bone?—as a child. My "patrol boy belt" I've called it ever since, just like another picture there, the treatment for that. I tell him about lab coats for cheap, half-price, in my new Lands' End catalogue. He's interested.

Back to the tables. One group is suddenly friendly—two students working together, two of the foursome on the thick-skinned guy.

Wanna see what we found? says one. He's excited, tells me to place my hand on the scapula, feel its top edge—the spine—and its angled sides. Down then, to the split triceps, where tucked into the split is the huge radial nerve that innervates most of the complicated fierce and delicate moves of the arm. Sensory response too, I imagine. It's white and thick. In general, one of them tells me, you can feel arteries and veins—they're round (and here he inserts a tiny probe into one to prove that fact), while nerves are flat. But the radial nerve is so large, it *appears* round.

The other guy disappears for a few minutes to visit the other three tables and see their progress. Returning, brightly he says he felt like he was doing rounds: "Hello, Mrs. Robinson, and how are you this morning? Oh, not so well, I see . . ."

I like these two.

The bodies that are so still, so endlessly receptive, taking it, taking it. But when we move the thick-skinned guy so the triceps can be opened, his lower arm slips. It half rests, half drops down the side of the table. A sudden very human moment as if he had just adjusted himself, turned slightly in sleep, pleased with his dream.

My Pilates teacher, Gail Dodge, tells me about her cadaver experience in PT school. Suddenly hitting *metal* in the heart. A pacemaker! Buried in there, completely unexpected. And her comment: I just wish we had respected them more. She catches my puzzled look.

Oh, not that we did anything weird or funny with the bodies. It's just that I knew so little, if only I had understood more then, seeing and handling everything so closely, it would have had much more meaning.

I get that. But my worry: How to get past mere identification? Past the scavenger hunt feel of a dissection lab? How to let it all *sink in*? To let what we do, the human weight of it, fill in, slow, and pool. My theory is what I do notice—and recall a day later—will stick. But I mourn—

grieve—all the things I am missing by sheer ignorance, inattention, self-absorption, fatigue, plain stupidity, impatience.

A line on Grace Benedict's syllabus: "A drawing is a picture of your understanding. As one's understanding is usually flawed, so are our drawings."

I suppose that is solace, of a sort.

8/28   Life Drawing

Two hours, 14 drawings, some—most—with the blackest India ink and the thick bamboo brush. Fast. Still. Quick multiple poses of the same model, the older woman so generously here in spite of the small oxygen tank she brings with her.

My drawings are terrible. Sometimes edging over into okay. *Parts* okay. We work with ordinary crayon too. Yellow. Green. A very purplish blue.

Watch how you phrase the line, Grace Benedict tells us. Which means where you stop, I guess. Long. Short. What those breaks *mean*. So you *read* the drawing. And where you start does matter. But in particular *where you stop*. Poems, I think. The mystery of line breaks where silence is a kind of breathing.

I begin crayoning in bones and muscles I'm starting to know from cadaver lab. X-ray vision, I tell Grace. *Not* what we're supposed to be doing. But she nods.

I circle furiously inside all my rounded shapes too—hip, chest— something I saw others doing, especially Grace herself. Suddenly movement is at least implied. Some sort of energy.

This whole business of looking—and in both situations, the "lookee" is naked, without defense. The cadavers more covered actually, their hands and feet in soaked tube socks, their heads wrapped in damp towels. The cutaways of skin are carefully laid back where they were each end of the day to cover the ruins beneath. Meanwhile the live model in studio has nothing but her dignity, her indifference, her closed eyes when the pose is supine. I can see her figuring out what to do with her arms, her hands.

We lookers ready to draw are all clothed, safe, distant. The med students in their white scrubs, a uniform that both unifies and separates. A small army of *lookers,* in both large rooms intent—scalpel or pencil. Maybe it doesn't much matter which.

The med students *go after,* find, isolate, and name; it's buried treasure. The young artists—*respond,* says Grace. Look for negative space, curves, turns in the body to guide you.

Look at the model, Grace keeps saying, and *not* at your drawing.

Look at the world, I think, and not yourself.

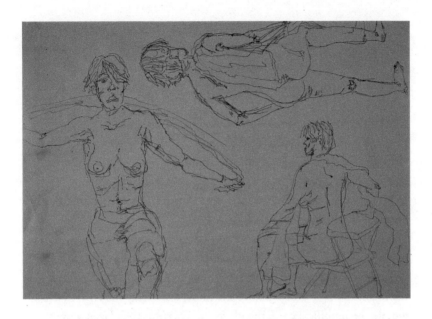

8/30–8/31   A Pause in All This! Labor Day Weekend

I talk to a rushed, overwhelmed, distracted Brigit on the phone, tell
her the two dangers in cadaver lab: that I get flooded with the technical
but vital minutiae, the physical details of it all, the Latinate names of
things, the pathways to recall, where nerves and arteries start, where
they end, etc. All that complex particular knowledge becomes an end in
itself. That I must remember I'm there to notice other things, oddities,
to absorb whatever comes my way. Second—I have to guard against it
growing too routine, too ordinary.

But that's the point, isn't it? she says. A remark that stops me. But
Brigit is right. This is a part of the tonal spectrum. And, of course, it's
against such a shrug that small aching things loom up and surprise. Or
maybe the ghoulish element is the default. No need to underscore. In
such strangeness, a great need to prize what *is* ordinary. The infamous
purpose of art, after all: to make the familiar strange, and the strange
familiar.

Something Will said on the phone yesterday about the construction of my hitchhiking memoir comes into what I'm doing here. Why did you write it, why now? Charlie Baxter's question last summer too. But that whole line of thinking gets larger: why write anything?

Maybe I'm looking for more mystery concerning the cadaver lab, a deeper question, and even the drawing I'm doing—putting myself into these situations to go silent and stare intensely. This particular, often larger, unnerving time on the wheel (dark of family, friends, self, all looming up and ahead) could be what launched this. One thing leads to another. Then even that thing vanishes.

A late note on the earlier embryo lecture. We see a film by and about Keith Moore—one of the authors of our thousand-pound textbook— obviously uncomfortable before the camera, showing the fetus in the womb, the umbilical cord, the placenta. He turns the placenta over and over, fetal side, maternal side. He lifts it back into the womb, small, glistening liver-colored, a pancake look-alike, the diameter about six inches. We see one for twins too, with two umbilical cords. He looks straight into the camera, speaking in a monotone. He doesn't wear gloves. Blood on his fingers.

The most surprising fact of Jim Walker's lecture: all embryos start out female, the default first take on the world, the grounding in that internal groove. I remember David saying that once.

Talk about getting launched *right*!

9/1   *Cadaver Lab*

The axilla. The armpit—a lurking immense tangle of nerves, blood vessels. And the lymph nodes (like black peas, our teacher says). It's one line branching many ways off the main pipeline of nerves, of blood; the lymph vessels are too small to see.

The moment comes to turn the cadavers, to put them on their backs.
The arms are stretched out straight—as straight as possible. Rope is cut,
and we tie the wrist to the table, both wrists, after pulling the arms down
slowly, a surprisingly long and delicate process because we could break
the bones easily. Unsettling, the two ways to see this. Either they are
tied down for torture or crucifixion, or they're released, opened up, arms
extended to embrace the world. How you see that defines *you,* doesn't it?

Their heads are still wrapped in wet towels, but in the case of one—
a female—the soaked sheet has slipped down, the genitalia revealed.
The men, their sheets start at the waist.

Suddenly one of the female med students says, Isn't it always like this?
The guys get covered, the women stripped down?

I think numbly of that infamous celebrated 19th-century painting by
Manet—*Le Déjeuner sur l'herbe*—two elegantly appointed men at a
picnic under trees beside a female. Of course she's naked as if, ho hum,
the usual, there for the taking. I remember she looks directly at the
viewer.

The students lift their lancets and do the same cuts they managed in
the back, now down the center, under the neck, stopping when the ribs
stop, retracting big squares of skin. Off go the breasts, as if we just *wear*
them. They cut and lift the deltoid.

In the busy triangle of the armpit, the many strands of vessels—nerves—
lie just under to speed the news to the muscle, which makes the arm move.
All to pick up a cup. Throw a pot in a ceramics studio. Wash the dead.
Paint the ceiling of the Sistine Chapel. Write a bad poem or a good one.

9/2   Life Drawing

We are drawing our teacher first, imagining the skeleton under her
jeans, her shirt, her boots as she poses with a shovel or simply raises her

arms. This requires x-ray vision of everyone. She presents a model of a skeleton and points out the curves—spine, femur, and the joints of shoulder, arm, pelvis, knee, elbow, ankle. The turns, the ball and socket links. I volunteer the wonderful names of C1 and C2: atlas and axis.

Then we do blind contour drawings with a new model, this one arriving late, a student. *Contour* means one never looks at the paper. So all my drawings turn even more bizarre—a Picasso cartoon, the special bits haywire and utterly peculiar. I keep going for the arm, the hand. In the end, on one large sheet, I find I've tried that arm and hand seven times, the foot, five times.

Grace says: connect them. I use dotted lines, like in a treasure map. I use curved lines and fiercely angled ones. In the last drawings, I do sketches rather than contour lines, looking at the paper allowed now.

To go into the lab—three weeks into this—is to be overcome by the smell of embalming fluid. I can't get it out of my scrubs or my lab coat. In fact, washing them with my clothes at home *spreads* it, like an infection. Everything reeks then, our shirts and jeans, towels right out of the dryer. I have to wash everything twice more.

First look, now that the cadavers are on their back: both women lie there, their sheets pulled down, their pubic hair revealed. How *personal* hair is. Of course the pubic hair, but even the wiry low growth on the chests of the men, the thick-skinned guy especially. The 100-year-old's body is so much like my grandmother's, and now her skin is a very dark pink, shiny from the moisturizing spray.

We are moving down the arm. The biceps skinned and revealed, lying on the humerus, are beautiful. Even Jim Walker says that. Mainly he keeps his wonder for the most curious things, "funky" in their tangle, in their odd shape or movement.

Two students practice their axilla presentation on me. (Hey, what's your name again? Oh yeah, Marianne. Can we practice on you?)

I'm listening. You know your stuff, I tell them right after. You guys are hot, I say.

It's the lights—my favorite of the two, pointing up at the intense hanging lamp above us. But they are all business, rattling off nerves, blood vessels, bones, muscles where all originates or inserts. They *do* rattle off, using no notes but reminding each other over the breaks in memory, in the pauses, in order to get through.

The arms of the cadavers keep wanting to fly up. I help tie down the right arm again. Someone's made a very poor slipknot, and I try to tighten it. Meanwhile the folds of the cut skin pulled back seem like ordinary insulation strips in an old house to keep out the cold; human fat's yellow like that stuff of spun glass one is never supposed to touch while thickening the attic walls, fearing multiple fiendish splinters.

Think ahead when I'm talking, one of the presentation guys tells his partner.

We get to the cubital fossa—*fossa* meaning pit—the concave middle space where the arm is a lever. The arteries, even the veins, are long and thick and amazing. Who knew?—the ulnar nerve, passing on the inward side, is the famous funny bone.

9/5   Cadaver Lab

Below the cubital fossa, the forearm—front side—and now the astonishing hand. Jim Walker's lecture takes a long time. David tells me before class nearly a fourth of the motor cortex is concerned—no, dedicated—to hand functions. And all the multiple-nerve pathways illustrate why.

In the lab, my bleaching and soaking the smell out of my scrubs and lab coat seem almost to work. It's easier to wear such things now, though the air in the lab is as overpowering as usual.

Two buckets-o-spinal-cords on the front table now, for some reason. The students rerope the arms of the cadavers, tie them back again. It's hard to get at the forearm, angle it up, for probing and cutting. Now revealed, the hand curls tightly, its soaked discolored sock finally removed.

In every case—*startling*! Of course more personal than the heretofore most personal thing about these cadavers: their hair—pubic and on the chest, the arms. The nails have darkened, as has the skin of the hand, though much of the body remains pale or even pink. In one wild moment, I notice the 91-year-old wears *nail polish*! No, I mean those acrylic stick-on nails that don't quite reach to the base of the real nail.

(Have the nails been growing after death? Like what Walt Whitman claims about human hair?)

A classy lady, says the seemingly most fashionable female med student. Is her remark ironic?

What color *is* that? I ask. It's a very rich dark red.

I don't know, she says, but I like it. Her seal of approval. Then later it comes to her, and she takes me aside: *Rouge Noir.*

Suddenly I reimagine this woman who has willed her body to us. Red stick-on fingernails—on a corpse! She's the pinkest of all four, a shiny dark pink. She's small overall, but her breasts are round and large. They have cut through her chest; each breast is perfectly centered on a flap. One keeps traveling, the breast set down by who knows who on her thigh, then later, when the handy *Human Atlas* takes that spot, it's balanced on her right knee. It's unsettling and almost comic to see this square-o-breast resting so *elsewhere* on the body, as if rearranged in a Picasso drawing, a blind contour attempt like the sort Grace had us doing the other day. The students work on, apparently oblivious to this small surreal touch.

One of the talkative presenters announces he knows *who* his cadaver is, the thick-skinned guy, 74 years old: I saw his obit in the paper last July. Said he was donating his body to the IU Med School.

No you did *not,* pipes in Jim Walker. Not *this* guy. They soak for six months, couldn't be him. Besides, they use many cadavers—for the dental school, the med school in Indianapolis, and in many regional locations like ours. *This* guy—*not* that guy.

He was a farmer, says the student. But okay. This isn't that guy.

Each group must choose a digit of the hand to skin. Three of the four go for the index finger. The last group narrows in on the one in the middle. I see you've picked "the finger with attitude," I tell them.

Yeah, the bird finger, someone calls back.

It's amazing, the hand's palm so deeply protected with its thick layer of fascia, everything—skin, surface vessels—welded to it, no give like the back of the hand has. Or virtually all other parts of the body really. A vast tangle of nerves coming down to the hand from the forearm, branches unto branches, the blood vessels too. Dizzying. Impossible nerves! Layers on layers of muscles attached at odd angles for various intricate movements of which the hand is capable. It will do its fine work.

I believe it now: a fourth of the motor cortex in charge of the hand—no wonder. The creases on the palm *track* those movements, the so-called life line, the heart line, etc. I read in the textbook that children with Down syndrome have only one line, breaking the palm in half.

As for those acrylic nails, pasted on the 91-year-old: how could they possibly have stayed on, six months floating in the embalming fluid? We ask Professor Walker about that.

Funny, he says. Mine keep falling off. How does she do it? The students look up. Delighted.

No, he grins. Mainly that fluid is water anyway.

No alcohol, I say?

Some. But not enough to work on these nails.

So the nails remain, brave frivolous detail of a life lived *how she wanted*. Reminds me of Anton Chekhov's journal notes: "They undressed the corpse but had so little time. A corpse with socks." Or was it gloves?

I'll have to find the book and check that. One of her hands is tied back with rope looped around the thumb. So it opens.

9/9   Life Drawing

The young model clearly loves artifice—pubic hair shaved, parts pierced in secret places (left nipple, genital region, but the standard lip and ear too). So much time and energy and pain, thinking about the body, its effect on others. A postmodern young woman.

Her hair—wild, semishort, falling tangled and straight out and down— is the most interesting thing to draw. I still *sketch*—much to Grace's disapproval. I can't help it. We work with ordinary pen on newsprint, and *block* our drawing. Which is to say, so much room for the head, a line where shoulders start, where arms and hands end, where navel lies, where the pelvic bones kick in, knees, ankles, etc. It helps. My drawings are gaining proportion.

Meanwhile, scissors for a new assignment. I race home on my bike at the break to get a pair—two pairs, in case someone else forgot. We're asked to cut the colored paper as if we were *drawing* the figure. Mine turns out okay: it's the tangled hair that gives it life, and the way she stands, slightly skewed.

Very nice, says Grace, I like the hair.

Funny. You *can* run with scissors—or at least race back with them on a bike.

Then: how to *sight*. All those students holding their pens in the air, against some point of the model, measuring. Grace explains it to me when I ask about the habit. Puzzling. My doing it seems pure theater. I just don't get it.

Someone else did forget. My second pair of scissors to the rescue!

Dorsal hand—the back of the hand—and the forearm. And the many kinds of joints. Also the morning of the group photo, which they drag me into though I try three times to resist. I have no business here really.

Now the hardest thing to do with some of the bodies is to turn the arm palm down. But it is really easier to skin the back of the hand than the front. No thick adhering fascia that the palm carries but loose skin instead. Revealed—the strange tendons, end straps of major muscles attached to the final edge of those from the forearm and strung across the knuckles up into the fingers. All this time, I thought those tendons were the actual bones, perhaps a common misconception.

I announce Grace Benedict's opening reception for the show of her paintings. Two students later ask more about it. One is an artist herself, she admits, as she "cleans up" the hand, scraping random fat off bones and tendons. She talks of her favorite medium—watercolor. Then we're onto birds. Talking birdsong above a cadaver! Our favorites: the wood thrush, late afternoons in nearby Horticulture Park, the chickadee anytime, anywhere. Plus all those other early morning and suppertime calls in the woods.

I was mobbed by a mockingbird once, says her partner on this team of two. I was a little kid. Never got over it. So says this confident young woman.

The hand is all about finding the buried nerves. The radial (near the thumb), ulnar (little finger side), and median (center, sort of), which plug in all muscles—moves, sensory news—to light them up. And the arteries and veins under the thick fascia.

All three of us look down and admire the cadaver's dark red nails again. But the index finger, right hand is normal, not prettied up. That's probably where the hospital nurses put the pulse ox, one says. So the phony nail on that finger wore off fast.

By the end of the session, the arms on all the cadavers are used to it, I think. Every arm stretched open. No ropes needed.

A bit I cherish, the only *non*-mouthful, *non*-Latinate phrase here so far: *the anatomical snuffbox*—the small triangle between two tendons, at the posterior (dorsal) base of the thumb. I explain it to a couple of groups, the whole *snuff* reference, acting the part, raising my bony hand to my nose for a big pretend inhale. Being as 19th-century-old-codgerish as I can, *Ah yes, finally my beloved snuff!* I say in my phony British accent. The students near me half smile, shake their heads.

The fact is I want to rename everything. More down-to-earth ones like the ye olde snuffbox! What a relief that would be.

9/11 *Life Drawing*

A male model for the first time, very moving somehow. He's somber, steady, startling to draw. We work with Conté crayon, going for quick drawings to capture streaks of motion. Thirty-second poses, one after another, all different positions. The harder part—after some sketchy pen drawings—another challenge. Respond to the exact same poses but use S curves or plain curves, long sweeping lines *only*. My default is that sketchy, hesitant, poor think-again-about-it thing. The clarity of one curved line seems miraculous, freeing, comic and serious at once.

Comic—as in it *releases.* Serious—as in it tightens, *insists* somehow. On one page I have a sketchy figure. Next to it, the S-curved one.

Connect them somehow, says Grace.

So I do a thought-bubble thing—the complex, sketchy guy *thinking* of a simpler self who is surrounded by a thought-bubble circle, little standard zeros leading to that outline from the head of the sketchy guy.

It took a while. I kept wondering whether really it should go the other way, the simpler figure dreaming the more complex guy. If I were younger, I suppose I'd go for that. A wish for depth, experience, more layers. As it is, the depth of that simple figure charms and interests—and age *wants it back*.

A connection to poetry seems somewhere in this curious comparison, later work vs. earlier work.

But exactly how, and why?

As for the cadaver lab on the other side of campus: What are we doing in that room? Are we simplifying, making clear and emphatic by diminishing the body, taking parts away?

9/12   Cadaver Lab

The hand surgeon comes up from Huntington, West Virginia, to ask the students questions. The honest-to-god Socratic method, rapid-fire, exhausting.

He's concerned most with *branching,* says Jim later. This nerve under *that* nerve to what other nerve under *which* vein, artery, around *which* bone. Most amazing to me, the major nerve—median—starting way up at the shoulder (from C7, say) stops cold at the middle knuckle of the middle finger. It's lateral nerves on the side that take up the work to arrive at the fingertip.

A thought about the body over time . . . Not the great structural genius I always thought. More like those ancient cities—one civilization built upon the previous one, rational but skewed, even muddled. Why would C7, for instance, send a nerve down to the third finger, or L5 connect all the way to the lower leg? Endless branches, seemingly wayward. The systems built *onto, into* other systems, like those human sites that grew slowly, over decades and even centuries. Parts that take over for other parts, unincorporated villages now into suburbs. Driving 30 minutes for orange juice no more! Or some beloved house, so badly wired then rewired but the lights still blinking.

9/16　*Life Drawing*

A clothed model, tall thin young woman in skirt and leotard top. We do the hard work of cutouts and, as usual, I'm best with the head, hair, even facial features, and very bad with most everything else. My scissors do it—pull and ravel/unravel.

We use the Conté crayon then, pressure on the "high" spots—x-ray vision would make these the denser moments of the figure, perhaps where underlying bone and muscle kick in.

No lines at all! Grace insists.

I circle too hard with the small crayon and gradually my hand, particularly my middle finger, goes numb. I think *median nerve.* It's odd to be working with a clothed model, though earlier and briefly we did draw Grace in her blue jeans and shirt.

But our moments of this seem so much less meaningful—not *seeing*, not being able to follow the full body line. Was it Grace's need for models that decided her agreement to a clothed session? Not that I blame this young woman. I'd be the same way, wanting to keep covered. Yet it does dictate a different relationship, clothes making the experience more distant, more publicly acceptable.

Which is to say, not sacred, forbidden ground at all. Not private, now without the tension and energy of the secret. We aren't trespassing. In theory we are seeing and recording what anyone might see.

9/17   Cadaver Lab

The thoracic wall, an easy lab, Jim says.

So it's the bone saw again, the smell of bone burning, the body's smoke. The med students wear goggles and in some cases face masks. Where to cut: as lateral as possible, then at the jugular vein, then about seven ribs down.

The big guy is the worst. It takes a long time for them to get through him. But care is needed—not to cut what shouldn't be cut—arteries, nerves. Not the soft tissue either, the diaphragm, etc.

I watch the rib panel loosen, and gradually they are able to lift it like a hinged lid to reveal the lungs. Pinkish, grayish, freckled darkly: one larger, one smaller.

Press here, someone says. Feel the air pockets underneath.

They're both relatively small, Jim informs us. In death, the pulled-in air forces the diaphragm way up into the chest, then always an exhale. The dying breath, I think. *The death rattle.*

In one cadaver, the woman with her red nail polish, the right lung is collapsed, wet, torn, oozing. One student steps away. I'm going to be sick, she says.

They use turkey basters to suck out the liquid—pink watery yogurt, another student says. She died of pneumonia, another tells us.

Later, from David: She drowned. That's what pneumonia *is*.

It's the first time I see the students freaked, flinching. Dr. Walker! they cry. But for some reason, this is one rare moment he isn't here. He's vanished. They bring the unflappable Samar Khirallah over, who is clearly unnerved.

Look, someone says. Even Samar's grossed out. This is bad.

Meanwhile, the other lung seems fine. That's strange, I say. No, it's not, a voice corrects me. They function quite separately, and there's a blood border, independent compartments in the chest wall.

Maybe she had cancer and part of this bad lung was removed, adds someone.

They recoil again, sucking up ooze with the turkey baster, staring into her chest, then looking away. It's the with-it female med student, the toughest one, usually aloof and steady, who's most alarmed.

Earlier, the breast on the chest flap was set to the left of this cadaver, on the table. Her perfectly round ample breasts, even after death's dehydration. I see the wiry white milk ducts making their way to the nipple, arriving eventually.

Breasts are just glorified sweat glands, our teacher said in lecture. Startled, I turned to a couple of female students—not very glamorous, is it?

9/18   Life Drawing

Grace Benedict says: Look   Think   Make a mark.

I put this together with Jim Walker's constant dictum: *Identify Appreciate   Move on*. In drawing class: *leave something behind*. In cadaver lab: *leave no trace*.

We have the uncensored live model back, the young woman pierced in her places. We continue the high-point density, press-down drawings, and then the robot geometric drawings (use no curved lines!), which I'm beginning to like a lot.

I want to *hear* you doing these, Grace said. She means the incisive hit of the single line. Its quickness. Eye to hand. The sound of that.

I'm more careful with my wrist, my numb finger and thumb at the root of it all.

9/22   Cadaver Lab

Still on the lung. An easy lab today, says Jim again. We take the lungs out and *appreciate* them.

He's right. It's not hard, but in the big guy, both lungs are huge. And students fight to get a grip on one, its edges, wedge it this way and that, the stretching and sucking sounds. Then, it's out. (It's a boy! I say, as they laugh.) Then they go back to the other one.

Beautiful, how the lobes of the lungs fit so perfectly together. One young man stands there amazed, taking them apart, putting them back, this soft-edged velvety jigsaw puzzle.

The thoracic cavity: we rarely fill it, even in the deepest breath. In none of the cadavers is the lung darkened fully though all are mottled some (clearly not smokers, says Dr. Walker, just the normal nasty stuff we all breathe).

The crap, he means, says a student to me in a whisper.

Someone shows me the tiny, nearly too-small-to-see air bubbles in the tissue of the lung. Walker asks that they cut down an inch or so

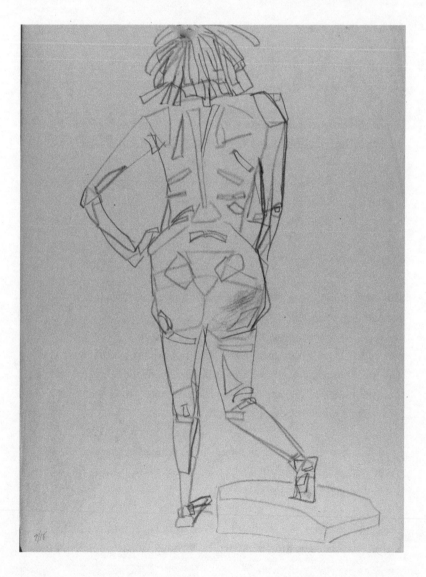

to "identify and appreciate" the vessels there. Two lungs, completely unconnected. Hence transplants are possible. A single collapsed lung *not* the end of the world. One with its *cardiac notch*. One with the *aortic groove*. The left smaller than the right.

The other bodies, beyond the big guy, have lungs of various sizes. The red-fingernail lady's one lung is diseased, says Jim. He's nodding over her pneumonia. They are still sucking out fluids.

The bronchi are tiny urgent trees, exploding sideways and down.

9/23 *Life Drawing*

The modest young woman in her long skirt again. We do cutouts, a task for me now. I've lost my fondness for them. I'm down to doing parts— head and shoulders, the legs, the feet. The internal cuts are the hardest, wielding my thin scissors into the paper. A slow business.

Second hour. Again the male model arrives, drops trou, is offhand, matter-of-fact up there. A few female students seem completely charmed all over again; they smile, almost giggle at his sweet taking orders from Grace about his pose, arm this way, leg that way. He is a pleasure to draw, all the musculature clear, the bones—collar, iliac crest, ribs, etc. Thin and muscular. And once more, immensely cheerful, this guy, like he's thinking glad thoughts about everything he's been given. Yet it must be odd for him, hearing Grace point out to us that shadow on *the* hip, that curve on *the* bicep, as if no longer his. We're still on the block-robot way of building a drawing, but we're allowed curves now, allowed *sketchy,* sort of.

The foreshortened thing is the worst, the angle where he's, say, lying down, his feet toward me, and to get that down right. It's perspective though not exactly. It's something else, more difficult. A godlike vision, impossible. Or a raven's, above and on the loose. In one, I've finally drawn a decent closed hand. That's thrilling.

Grace asks: Are you drawing in the cadaver lab? You should be.

Not allowed, I tell her. No photographs, no drawings. (As if anything I'd sketch would even remotely *resemble* thus reveal who these four really were in life!)

9/25 Life Drawing

We continue with the Conté crayon, and one young woman, a model new to me, sits, stands, lies down—the works. Interesting, that so much is hidden in the female body by curves and—as the med students say—the sub-cu, all that fat lying underneath seemingly everything. Which may be why it's more intriguing to draw men, more in-your-face stark angles of muscle, tendon, bones, less subcutaneous tissue. Just more to see and draw.

I keep redoing, starting over. One seated version of her, then three on my rag paper page, all facing the same way. Horrible, these efforts. Yet in going back to this page with the three of them, filling it with the required background of lines to do this contextual thing Grace demands, I like the unfinished cartoonish look. Three muses? Or the three fates? Or, how many witches chant around that nightmare cauldron in *Macbeth*? Maybe these are sirens. Or just three badly drawn women.

Later, when I show David at home, I realize they age, going backward, right to left. Not their bodies so much. I see it in their faces. And the lines behind and surging put them at the beach or in water. Some impossibly mythic spot.

A late assignment during the last bit of class: do compartment drawing. A part of the figure, then another part, then the same part from a different angle. I use pen and ink. Always, the terrible feet I make. And hands. I keep trying to get those bones in the back, the S curve of the spine on which—Grace doubles down—everything depends.

Some continuing thoughts, differences and similarities ...

—Two classes of clothed people looking (mainly) at unclothed people.

—One group observes in a strict categorical way (*identify* vs. *look*!).

—A special, specific private site for both, closed doors in both cases. (You must knock and wait before entering, says the sign on the drawing studio.)

—Special clothes—a uniform in cadaver lab (scrubs, lab coats you never get the smell out of). Nothing that unordinary in the studio, just clothes you could ruin in an instant and not regret too much (ink and color spills, etc.).

—The whole point of the "lookees"—models to be stared at, somehow translated to paper in the studio; cadavers to be opened, probed, and "appreciated" before Jim Walker's urgent "move on!"

—But both models and cadavers are, in their way, disassembled. Both are profoundly appreciated.

—I take the elevator *down* into the basement and then walk through the catacomb-like corridor (for storage, for bringing in large equipment, a heavy door to open) to get to the cadaver lab. (I think: air lock, for outer space.) For drawing class, I ride *up* the huge freight elevator three floors to find the studio. In both there's

a wait, a vertical transformation, a weightlessness, the starts and stops of the elevator itself. In both cases, the thick metal doors open and discharge me.

9/26 Cadaver Lab

We change clothes. As usual, I hear the young women chat as I slip out of mine in a bathroom stall. Everyone is noting the terrible smell of the scrubs again. I hear: Do you think we will ever get used to it?

No, it gets worse, someone answers back.

In lab, they're already unwrapping the bodies, pulling back the chest flaps of skin, retracting the strips of muscle, lifting out the cut panel of rib, lifting each lung from its slick cavity and putting them aside, down on the thigh or on the lower abdomen. So again, each time this review of the way we've come.

Now, after so many days of this, it looks easy, puzzle pieces taken out
and put back, no memory of the confusing pile of such pieces all tied in
by tissue, fat, ligament, nerves, muscles. Those lungs again. On the big
guy, they sit to the side, still enormous. I touch one edge, the air pockets
still evident under the surface, a bit like liver-colored bubble wrap. Air
he actually once breathed? And this lab itself. You turn your head and
see another lung, sitting on the edge of the table.

Meanwhile they are cutting more slowly, through the thick sac in the
left lung cavity, snuggled toward the right. What protection! So much
packaging. The heart down a bit, at its famous angle. They cut the
enormous tubes *to* the heart and *out* of it too. "The great vessels" are, in
fact, truly great, monstrous, the aorta the largest, curving over the heart
like some sort of creature unto itself. The huge pulmonary arteries too.
And thick pulmonary veins entering the heart.

They are passing the big guy's around now. We all hold it for a few
seconds, this human heart. Like everything else about him, it's massive,
way bigger than the *fist* routinely described as its normal size.

Then the cleaning of the heart, taking the probe and poking out dried
capsules of blood lodged in the vessels. Soon there is a little pile of
crumbly bits. Jim Walker is watching. He suggests they take it over
to the sink and rinse it—rinsing the human heart!—to remove the
congealed particles inside. My gloves are bloody just from those few
moments holding it.

The other bodies have released their hearts too, none this size, of course.
The 100-year-old's is remarkably impressive though, a decent size, very
little fat on it. The smallest is a genuine fist—the pneumonia/fingernail
woman's heart. Bird-sized, for 91 years. Three of these people died of
some heart problem, we are told, but nothing seems untoward about
any of these.

Cut into, the hearts have that fascinating variation of tissue in their
chambers. Smooth inside (medial) wall lining vs. the much thicker

outside wall which, I assume, does the tireless pumping. The heart *is* a muscle, after all. It's deeply grooved, with small variegated curves, a maze really.

A pretty simple lab today, Jim says cheerfully. And soon, they are packing up the cadavers again, hearts first this time, then lungs, ribs, muscle, skin. They spray the bodies with the alcohol, fabric softener, and water mixture and lower the plastic shroud.

9/29 Cadaver Lab

Just lecture today. The origin of the heart again, in greater detail, the embryo's long tube which folds and refolds on itself to create chambers, then chambers *within* chambers. We are looking at slides. The whole morning a darkened room, the bright ancestral screen.

9/30 Life Drawing

The model overslept. Or had second thoughts. She's new at this, says Grace Benedict, who disappears to call her.

I chat about religion with the talkative one next to me who's about to student-teach at McCutcheon High School. I hate it, she says, when people try to convert me. We agree. The colossal nerve of that.

Meanwhile the model does not show. And will not, which becomes apparent by the minute. Grace jumps on the platform and leans against the narrow high table there, a kind of pillar. We draw her—four parts that can be repeated—in the blocks we quarter our big newsprint pages into. Charcoal Conté crayon, very soft and dusty, hard to get an edge. But it's not about edges, I remind myself.

The rest of the time: ditto and ditto, in parts and pieces. We take turns playing the model, with clothes, of course. The student teacher jumps in for her spell. But not before the sorority girl—so proud of that—takes her hit. She struggles to stay still and I can see it's painful, that she regrets her good-sport volunteering.

Anyone else? says Grace.

Lapsed-Catholic guilt overcomes me. I find myself leaping up, then slow down strolling to the platform. And you want me to . . . ?

You can sit, Grace tells me, and face any way you want.

I'm wearing a zipped sweater, quite baggy, and my black jeans, elbows on my knees, hands together, fingers interlaced, leaning forward. Too late I realize what that young woman probably did: I should have found a more comfortable position somehow. But I'm stuck: 10 minutes minimum. I close my eyes at least.

It's very disconcerting to hear them drawing all around me. I'm circled by that urgent, locked-in sound. When I do open my eyes, they seem serious, no expressions at all. From my own efforts at drawing, I know they are following all my angles, lines, curves, and it's—what? I'm hardly worth the effort of their effort, I think.

Subject and object, we are all verb, then a stillness.

10/6 Clouds, etc., by Plane

En route home! From a visiting poet week in Fairbanks, the university there, changing planes in Minneapolis, then back to Indiana—

Just a few thoughts about my Alaska talk, which meant my speaking out midstream, before any time for this experience to settle really, this cadaver lab/drawing class, this duality—life and death, the live models, the cadavers. And poetry, of course.

I told the MFA students in Fairbanks about putting oneself in odd occasions just to see what happens and, eventually, what poems might result. I read to them about the rib and lung, from this notebook. What's hard—I think this now, writing this—is to see, be able to recognize what really is, not what *should* be happening.

If you anticipate, can you be surprised?

10/7   Life Drawing

No class really. We're to stare at all our drawings, pick 20 for our critique Thursday, work on our cutouts. I make an appointment with Grace Benedict for that. It's a bit depressing and overwhelming: 20 drawings? My favorites? Or my most interesting, if embarrassing, screwups? Is there a difference?

It's the abdomen now. A "day of layers" as Jim Walker says. All the muscles from Pilates class we find in the dissection, revealed: Gail Dodge's continual citing of the psoas, the transverse, etc. The famously crucial and needy *core*.

In lab, it all comes back again, after the week away. The smell, the bodies as usual though the groups have been shuffled, new foursomes on each of the four cadavers.

Where do we cut? asks one young woman suddenly—for the first time looking helpless, holding her scalpel over this part of the belly, that part of it.

What does *The Dissector* say? Jim says.

Mostly, this time, it's about muscles—the transverse, the famed six-pack, for starters. Hey, this guy's a real "four-pack" anyway, someone says about the slighter of the two male cadavers. Or about the layers of skin, the deep fascia below the sub-cu (the so-called superficial fascia).

I'm lost in the fascia! one young woman cries out.

We find two hernias (you will see a lot of these in your time, Walker tells the students), one on the unhunky male, one on the 100-year-old female, both down at the groin. One has been repaired, I'm told, but I have no idea how they know this. I think of my mother, at 12, getting hers fixed on the family's dining room table in the '30s, no hospital yet in that tiny Illinois town. Or my old grandfather, born 1875, working his hernia *in* every morning at the edge of his bed, putting on his truss as my brother and I, fascinated and mildly horrified, watched in secret from the hallway.

But yes, so much sub-cu! Why is that? I ask Jim. Protection of the organs? Warmth?

Or just a lot of good eating, he says. Plus all of the above.

I'm standing around, telling Jim Walker how I quoted him in my Alaska talk: *Identify, Appreciate. Move on.* That last, he says, is most important. Then: They made T-shirts, you know, with that phrase on them. For the big test on Friday.

Yeah, says one of the med students, overhearing us, looking up from the 100-year-old. And we have one for you too, he tells me.

Really? I say. I can't believe it, the sweetness of this.

Later, he hands one to me, dug out of his crammed locker, amid falling shoes and books. Robin-egg blue, 100 percent cotton. *P=MD* on the front (They *hope* for that pass, Jim Walker had whispered), and on the back, his favorite phrase—*Identify, Appreciate. Move on.*—followed by their names and IU MED CLASS, 2012. It's all so dear.

Out of my scrubs and lab coat, I immediately put it on. Proudly. And wander down the hall, thanking them, whoever's in sight.

Kind of a weird color, isn't it? a student says.

Hey, I say, it's great! Worse would be bright orange or some awful yellow. And she agrees.

Earlier in the lab, I noticed for the first time an out-of-the-way cabinet with drawers marked *Tibia* and *Fibula Bones, Vertebrae,* and *Hands and Feet.* I'm guessing strays. Relics from another year, an earlier class. Think of it: a drawer of hands, a small colony of feet, so many bones at rest.

One thing more to recall: two young women, the tough one and the sweet one, poised over the nonhunk male cadaver—set to cutting out the penis in its cloud of gray-black hair. The two male students in their group pretend not to notice their discomfort, and chat together over the guy's head and shoulders.

The sweet one turns red when I ask her about it. Why are you two doing these cuts?

They refused, says the tough one, pointing to the guys who studiously ignore us. In a few minutes, by the sinks: they're big babies, the women tell me. Really. They couldn't do it.

The next day, seeing Amanda Curnock, my British doctor, about my poor ear, I tell her this story.

People get squeamy, she shrugs. Some can't bear to do certain parts in a dissection lab. The eyeball is big like that too. Some won't touch it. I tell her our cadavers' heads are still wrapped in soaked white towels.

Really? she says. In London, ours watched us the whole time!

10/9 *Life Drawing*

I look at all my drawings at home for the midterm critique and take them into class, laying them out on the floor in the hallway. My favorites among the pieces show (sort of) various required things: variety of line, density, tone, proportion, perspective, foreshortening, etc. But I'm unsure what some of those categories actually mean.

Grace Benedict is kind. My energy is lyric, she says. Original. Furious. She likes the lines. I tell her about the connections I'm finding between my approach to poems *and* the drawings. What I don't say is the excitement, the near terror of the blank page in both cases.

Here, she says, here you used the tool wrong. That's the problem. Not *how* you see. Just how you handle the Conté crayon. Go sideways. No line. No scribbling. Have patience.

10/10   *Cadaver Lab*

So we enter the abdomen. Just to *appreciate,* says Walker, hardly any cutting.

First, of course, the lecture, which includes the embryo's development, another long tube at the start, the "gut tube" this time, so much like the heart's beginning in its "cardiac tube" that will fold and refold. But the gut tube's folding includes all manner of wild herniation—looping out to make the loops that will be intestines, and then—amazingly—they are reabsorbed into the system. Buds off the tube form liver, gallbladder, pancreas. But that we all start so simple, a mere tube! Then it "goes to town" (i.e., crazy), as my grandmother liked to say.

This is the last day before fall break and the students are exhausted. They really work so hard. As I change into scrubs in the women's john, I hear them out there in the more public areas, changing their clothes too. I am so sick of this, one of them says.

Yeah, says another, I am so out of here!

In lab, cuts are made under the ribs (or where the ribs used to be), past the famous six-pack, which is to say, through the muscle. Retracted back, that tissue reveals all the intricate, crowded entrails. It's positively medieval, the beautiful, huge two-lobe liver; the spilling-out-bright-green gallbladder; the simple large colon ascending at the transverse and then descending; the busy smaller intestines that seem endlessly to loop and reloop, often lined on the outside with layers of fat, a glistening bright yellow. All this color! But to what end?

First—and this moves me beyond reason—there's the "greater omentum" under the muscle, under the fascia, the strangest almost-endearing apron attached to the top of the abdominal cavity where the ribs stop. Sub-cu embeds it to a greater or lesser degree, but in at least two of the cadavers, it's a simple garment, never attached at the bottom. One young man working with the fingernail-polish lady simply reaches in, both hands on that lower edge, and pulls it up—a veil, something off the altar—to reveal all the organs beneath.

Something about this stuns me. The veil itself is a thin expanse of mesh woven every which way, like chain mail—something, again, so seemingly medieval. Extra protection, almost magical, for those organs crucial to the body and its workaday functions. Small bits further amaze: the tiny appendix, a narrow pointed cone off the large intestine. Everyone is amused to find it at all and on the right side, legendary of course. A reverse witch's hat.

In one instance, as a student works, cutting through to the omentum, the cadaver's right arm has slipped up, crooked and raised as if to defend or attack, or simply to mourn as the students work to find vital nerves and arteries, meaning no harm.

There are pockets, places in the abdomen where fluids pool as we sleep. Our teacher discussed them in lecture. One—the *pouch of Morrison* on the right, below the liver; and you can reach in—I do, with my gloved hand—to feel, not to see yet. There's an opening, a *foramen,* that our guidebook *The Dissector* calls *Winslow* on the other side. I ask Jim about the names of things, how they've changed over time. Because yesterday, my friend, artist, and slide librarian for Art and Design, Kathy Evans, told me how earlier editions of *Gray's Anatomy* show wildly different names for things, those vessels and muscles.

Yes, says Jim, so many used to carry the surnames of doctors and anatomists who first identified them. All that's changing, but somehow *pouch of Morrison* and *foramen of Winslow* survive.

The big guy, as usual, is high drama, his large loops of intestines richly threaded with bright yellow fat. And as I watch one young woman explain—*present*—to Professor Walker what she's found (crucial nerves, the connecting ligaments, organ to organ, and so on) I think this: never have these bodies had such meticulous attention. Not in life. Never was anyone so fascinated by them. I think how my mother would have loved this depth of scrutiny, she who liked to say in old age "My social life is going to the doctor!"

10/15   Cadaver Lab

So we had a fall break. Big deal, a med student complains. Two days off.

But through that time, these organs, these livers, have waited. And the cheerful kelly-green gallbladders, and the stomach, which in the 100-year-old turns out to be a small misshaped tube high under the rib, near the heart.

I hold the big guy's liver. It's like those hard-foam fuzzy toys, the two lobes fitting perfectly together. Amazing. And speckled, in all these cadavers, though some darker than others. Did this guy drink? I ask Jim, given the shade of it.

He's silent for a moment. In fact, these livers, he says, look pretty good.

The pancreas is there, the spleen, all a bit enlarged, herniated off the embryotic gut tube long ago and reabsorbed into the thoracic cavity. Less fat around the organs in all these cadavers than I thought there'd be.

10/16   Life Drawing

The model is a no-show again. We take turns once more, drawing the figure, its secrets shrouded by most ordinary sleeves, pant legs, shoes.

I draw the sweet-faced 6'8" guy from class. He looks like a monster under my dodgy care.

10/17   Cadaver Lab

A visit from local celebrated surgeon John Francis, who speaks so quickly, I can barely follow. But I get this much: he loves his job. The kids are riveted.

His mission—teach the hands. It comes down to this, in spite of the expensive fancy machines and their testing. *Put your hands on the body.*

And there are simple commands for old traditional DIY tests, which begin

Cough

Swallow

Press outward

I want that list annotated, I say to Jim Walker later.

Me too, he says.

10/21   *Life Drawing*

The young woman with her hardware is back. We're allowed more minutes per drawing. I'm not sure time improves me much.

Still in the abdomen, next level. The kidney. The two women's are tiny.
One student, charmed with the fingernail-polish lady's, holds it high.
Adorable, he says.

But it really is. They cut it to reveal the pattern inside, the loops of
Henle like so many branching trees, right out of a page from a linguistics
text tracking a complex sentence, an old-fashioned diagram.

I remember the day we cut out the liver: a curious click or snap, a broken
sound. It's okay, said the student who did the cutting. We'll be doctors
someday. We'll know how to fix that.

Meanwhile, the male cadaver—not the big guy—has turned his head
sideways, his left arm flung out now, not in defense but seemingly
relaxed, open to all that has befallen him. The students chat on about
specialties they'll never want: anesthesiology, nuclear medicine,
pathology, urology, colon and rectal surgery.

Lower, in the 100-year-old, the thoracic aorta. Press this, says one young
woman. I do—a terrible cracking, like the vessel is lined with the oldest,
most brittle plastic that breaks under the slightest touch. I jump back.

That's plaque, she says.

10/24   *Cadaver Lab*

Now I am getting the days mixed up; they run together.

We go lower in the body. The anal cavity, the urogenital cavity. I walk
into lab to see the 100-year-old pulled down on the table, legs dangling
stiffly off the edge.

It's the rope again. And there's much ongoing talk about how to secure that rope, tied now around her ankles and flung over the water pipe in the ceiling.

I tell three young women about my grandmother's phrase about any gyno exam, a "turning up to the doctor." Samar grins, overhearing. Then: I hate this part, she quietly tells me.

The group works until they find the crucial nerve and the clitoris, which I've mispronounced all these years, hearing Jim Walker name it. Somehow humanizing and life-giving, this 100-year-old, the late 1920s, say, when—assuming if—she discovered it. Or someone she loved discovered it for her.

One guy, the quietest student looming over the fingernail-polish lady: I never want to do OB-GYN. No way.

I do hate this part, Samar says to me later. We try to be so respectful about the bodies, but this region . . . She shakes her head.

They've cut the penis in half at table one. Not the hunk's. Ouch, I say. They're sheepish and wise-guy curious by turns.

The high point, two days earlier: finding the sciatic nerve, running from and through the groin into the thigh. It's white, flat, thick, huge. Everyone's amazed. *Wows* all over the place, one and all.

11/11 Life Drawing

The young male model again, long drawings this time, only two in the whole class period.

I'm sketching too much, and the angle I choose—where to enter, what to cut, bring forward—bores even me. Blah. Virtually all in the anatomical position. What's nifty is how to color-tone paper, the sweeping quick slide of the pastel on thick white sheets (no rag paper now), and then the time it takes to grind such color (chalk really, these pastels) into the surface. There's aqua, orange. Green too. I use my Conté crayon for that.

The best part of the drawing is the crosshatched shadow to the right of the figure. My great discovery—I can sweep it out of its outline, hence *motion,* hence something in this dullest of drawings I've made—alive!

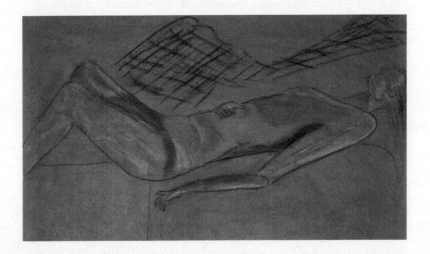

11/12   Cadaver Lab

I go to class, but the whole morning is for the exam. A major one, including identification in the lab itself, where Jim and Samar have isolated and tagged vessels, bones, regions, nerves.

My lame joke: in a previous class, I offered to take the exam too, to lower the curve and help *up* the scores of the students. Nope, doesn't work that way, Jim says, as if I was serious.

I talk only briefly to him in the hallway. About London and Edinburgh, where I'll be going for about 10 days, part of this fellowship. I mention the surgical museums in those places, and John Hunter, the "father of modern surgery," his famous comparative collection of bodies, parts of bodies, animal and human. Jim nods. Says he has an article or two on the guy.

Eventually, every student in class must give a 10-minute article presentation, and they are signing up for slots. I say I'm willing to bring in some information about John Keats, the poet famously trained to be a physician in London. Great, says Jim. We have time.

Seems doable enough. And, I hope, not a trap I've set for myself. But I do have small prints of a 19th-century dissection to give out as party favors. And poems touching on injury with a medical eye—among them work by Sylvia Plath, Lucia Perillo, my brilliant late colleague Tom Andrews, Keats himself, of course, and the good Doctor Williams.

11/13   *Life Drawing*

Bingo. Finally a decent drawing! And *color* again. What a wonderful lift to this day. I really do love color-toning the paper. Having more choice now, having bought several NuPastel options for exactly this—a rich violet, blue, red, yellow, green.

A revelation: *the eraser* is a drawing tool.

After laying down a charcoal-pencil-faint outline of the figure (the young pierced-everywhere woman again), I go in with the pencil-sharpened eraser to take out the lighter spots. Later I go into those moments again, adding cooler colors against the darker violet that is my background basic color tone, what I worked in earlier by hand. Warmer colors—slashes of yellow, of the orange Conté crayon—is where I blur with my finger.

Or, as Grace tells me, use another kind of eraser for that. It will have a different effect, though on the subject of finger action, there's this from Grace: I assign each digit a different color. Useful advice. Saves trips to the sink to wash my hands. Then the darker pastels—the deeper blues or the green—are kept separate for the more shadowed areas.

What's astonishing, for starters, is to give, then take away, then give again. The eraser as a tool *to make a mark*. Exactly like revision in a poem.

Grace: You draw what you see *and* you draw what you imagine.

Later, watching people talk at Don Platt's reception for the wonderful poet Van Jordan, who is here on campus for a reading, I keep seeing how parts of their faces are lit, part in shadow. And if I were to draw them? How quick I'd be, erasing this bit or that as the running commentary takes place on whatever color-toned paper. Dark blue, I'd make the background.

Contrast, says Grace, unto mantra.

Tension is what makes beauty, I tell my poetry students. I mean it's what makes meaning.

11/14   *Cadaver Lab*

The moment is huge: the day the heads are unwrapped. Off with the soaked towels.

But first, Jim Walker's lecture on head and neck, all the valleys in the bony concave of the skull, the holes in that bone where nerves and blood vessels thread, the layering of skin, dura mater, bone, sub-cu, the two sources of innervation, C_1–C_8, and the brain stem, out of which true cranial nerves emerge.

As usual, I am skimming the surface, barely holding on. Clearly this is Jim's favorite turf, his baby, the place in the body he most happily engages and sheds his light for us.

Break. And a second break. That's how much there is to talk about. And we're not even really touching on the brain itself. That's next term, in Neuro, says Walker.

Finally it happens. We change into our scrubs and enter the lab. But I've already missed it: the actual unwrapping! They've just taken off the towels, and there they are: four faces, turning these cadavers into human beings.

How even to write about this. They're stunning, beautiful, darkly radiant, so heart-stopping particular and individual. Here we were, all term, so far into every corner of their bodies with probe and lancet, nosy as hell, curious and meticulous and amazed into the most private of places. Yet. It's only *now*—with their faces—that they seem human, with separate lives, childhoods somewhere back there, memories of afternoons, of evenings, years of sleep and dream, hard work, sorrow, deceit, remorse, joy, pride, indifference, anger.

I can't get those faces out of my mind—the only time I wanted to draw them. But my skill would fail them. They *are* beautiful. Old faces, a lifetime in each one.

—The petite, large-breasted, fingernail-polish woman, 91 years old, her face small, immensely delicate, eyes closed, still pink, her skin tone.

—The smaller man, squared face, much resolve, eyes closed too.

—The big guy, the cadaver pinup. His head—not surprisingly—huge, thick neck, nose, lips, forehead, cheeks, everything large, all judge-like, sober, definitely a great character-actor face, like those pictures of Theodore Roethke, Clarence Darrow, someone out of Dickens. Or he's powerful in a classic-movie kind of way, serious, set.

—And my favorite, my charm, the endearing enduring 100-year-old. Her mouth gapes open as if she's crying out her silence. Her dentures long gone, her face cocked back, eyes open. She's the most beautiful. I touch her cheek. Oh, to wish her well into the next life, over those mythic waters.

All have their heads shaved. The men's whiskers are apparent, a gray fuzz on both. Does the hair grow after death, as Walt Whitman says? I finally ask Jim that.

No, he says. But the skin shrinks, and so it seems that way.

Everywhere the students are at work, hands on the circular saws, the smell of bone seared, a kind of smoke in the air though not quite a haze.

First they carefully cut the scalp on the head, the very top, making a cross to pull and peel back the four sections to reveal the bone surface of each skull. Then the saws—their noise and dust and scent. The cutter in surgical mask and protective glasses in case any bone bits fly. They follow a thick marker line that's been made—purple for the 100-year-old, blue for the big guy, yellow for our small fingernail woman, green for the other guy. They cut and cut, circling the skull.

Not deep, Samar warns. Don't cut the brain!

The sound of bone breaking. They lift the top of the skull with a tool that pries. And there it is, the brain itself, all its spirals and squiggles, resting with such elegance. To lift that out is a complicated business. Jim and Samar aid here since cutting the nerves and vessels without damage to the brain is key.

I pick up each skull bowl, all four. Thick-walled layers because there was a world within to defend, to protect.

And now the brains are lifted out carefully, the students dumbfounded. We pass around the brains, take them in our cupped hands, admire each like a new baby, as we did with the hearts.

I hold two—the regular guy's first. Then, for a longer time, the 100-year-old's. I ask Jim then: So can we hook this one up to a screen now? And watch her hundred years of memories roll out?

I hold her brain stem then, her USB drive. And the port? At the base of the brain, its swirls turn most delicate, into the thinnest spaghetti.

People are quietly jubilant. *This is so cool,* I hear over and over. We *witness.* And know deep reverence for a moment.

Each brain is then placed in a gallon plastic bucket with its yellow lid marked Cadaver 1 or 2 or 3 or 4, with the term and year scribbled in, Fall 2008. They will be dissected next term.

Meanwhile Jim is busy pointing out the moonscape of the vacant skull—the holes for vessels, the depressions for this and that, the clear airy expanse in there now. And the skin flaps at those corners of cut scalp—folded down and back, the two forward ones lying over their eyes now. To blindfold. To give them privacy, I like to think. Someone has placed a large red rubber band around those flaps to secure them.

It's then that I notice the silver medallion with its number on each earlobe, attached by a metal clip.

Well, says Jim to me, a lot of poems here, right?

It's amazing, I say. They're so beautiful.

Yeah, but soon we'll be taking off those faces. So stare while you can, Jim tells me.

Then the students are wetting paper towels, dampening down the inside of each skull, stuffing in those towels so they almost look intact, these faces, these heads, their brains across the room floating in each opaque bucket.

To return to those faces still stuns. They've been coming at me at odd times all weekend. They're like charcoal drawings, their skin intricately lined, darker in those lines, so much shadow built right in. Like those haunting Renaissance drawings in the old elephant folios in the most hidden aisles of the library. Again, profoundly beautiful.

Today it's the eye, and the students chisel back the top-right corner of the skull's interior to find the optic nerve and all the other cross-hatching vessels. A hard job. They chip with a blunt plastic hammer and small chisel, the eye being part of the brain, connected by the optic canal.

It's here I really wish again that I could draw the faces of the cadavers, and the students too, so profoundly absorbed, the one who taps and chisels and those who gather around her to watch intently under the circle of hanging light. All faces are lovely.

Meanwhile, the front flaps of the scalp drape forward once more, covering each cadaver's eyes as the students pound and chip and talk.

On the petite fingernail woman, a student takes his probe and pries open one eye. Blue! he says, as if discovering an inland sea. She was classy, he announces, the guy who peeked and reported early on the big cadaver's face, declaring him a farmer, no one to mess with.

So many nerves and vessels coming out and into the skull's bony compartments. A busy place. Confusing. The students despair, their task to see the top of the eyeball at least, down below this bony inner wall, down beyond all the nerves they dare not damage. And the eyes—unlike lungs—are connected, deeply. In lecture: shine a light in one pupil, the other responds too.

We learn about tears in lecture, the "lake" at each corner of the eye, and the small, funny but thoroughly reasonable name—the *puncta*—for the tiny hole there that takes back some of those tears, routes them through the nasal passage into the throat.

That's why you're blowing your nose when you cry, says Jim Walker. That's why you keep swallowing hard.

Swallow your sorrow, I think. Or your joy.

Always the eye is washing itself, a constant maneuver. But tearing up— what *is* that about? I ask our teacher. Why do great sudden shifts of emotion start up this curious machinery?

He agrees it's the emotional center in the brain that kicks in and sends the message to the tear ducts to start up, to let loose. But why?

It must be a protective mechanism, I think. But what are the tears protecting? Why is the *eye* at risk in grief, or in utter happiness?

The students chip and pound and clearly *appreciate* those intricate wirings, eye to brain and back again. Eye *as* brain.

11/18   Life Drawing

Hands and feet. So why is the model before us in her altogether? She might as well be in shorts, in a T-shirt. But there she is, a first-time model minus her clothes trying to appear as blank and indifferent as possible.

The hands—so difficult. The feet, even harder. I'm the only one who color-tones the page dark blue before starting. Because I love the sweep, the brilliance. And I work the eraser—it makes me more alert to what is light and what is dark. (So revising makes me see more clearly too? I hope so.)

Hand. Hand. Hand. Foot. Hand. Last on that page, a giant foot. Big Foot, I say, a dumb joke to my compatriot at the next table.

But how odd the hand really is. No balance, it seems. No symmetry. Bones evident in the rise of knuckles, the shadows there. Such a curious shape to it.

Be careful of your edges, Grace tells me. Shadows—and cross-hatching. That elegant smudging—only on one side. Make it clear, she says.

The thumb is a lovable oddity. The fingers, delicate yes-men, yes-women. And the little finger trails off to almost nothing in its own cloud of being.

Keep looking, says Grace.

And she's right. I think I'm finished, then stare again, and find some amazing rise of bone, some shallow, some line I haven't noticed. It all keeps opening.

My major discovery, really a rediscovery—the great *swoosh* that I can do with the side of the black Conté crayon, sweeps to get the overall structure, the energy of hand or foot. I do this on the second plain white sheet, no color this time. And then draw in more intricate bits.

A genuine release. But a charcoal stick would be a better *swoosh* choice, easier to erase.

I like that, says Grace, seemingly surprised by the foot I've made, the hand that clenches and holds on for dear life. You've loosened up, she declares. Good.

How peculiar this is. A whole roomful of hands—drawing hands!

11/19   Cadaver Lab

It's all about the ear today, and my own are hurting, just listening to the lecture. Endless stream of nerves involved, how we are to go in from the inside of the skull, very much how we entered the eye's fiefdom earlier.

The ear's territory is one segment down in that bony expanse, that empty curve that once housed the brain. We can't see it yet, but so many small empty spaces in the skull—to lighten the head, Walker says.

These blank spots in the body fascinate. In the head, they're sinuses, of course. No fancy pouch of whomever this time. Another cool thing is the small muscle—the tensor tympani—which blunts loud sounds automatically to save our hearing.

This ear business. The hardest bone in the skull, Walker tells us. It's true, because in lab they are doggedly chipping away to invade the ear's small quadrant. Imagine a room, our teacher says, using his "little person walking there" imagery to make it real, more memorable. The hard part here is the force needed to remove the bony wall, to enter that space. But beware: it's that very force that destroys. Those tiny mechanisms—incus and malleus and stapes. The drum itself. So easily missed, smashed by the chisel and plastic hammer. For the group working on the fingernail-polish lady, this suddenly happens. They're sick at heart, starting again on the other side, the other ear.

Wanna see these? says one of my favorite students. She's holding up small glass vials, tiny bony bits in the bottom. Little incus and malleus and stapes from some long-lost cadaver. How many semesters have the pieces languished there in silence, these brilliant little gizmos for picking up sound. I think of those intricate carvings we saw in the British Museum—a Cecil B. DeMille cast-of-thousands miniature rendering of the Crucifixion, say, done in the Middle Ages, dug into the side of a walnut. Something like a walnut, probably a shrunken oak burl.

On the male cadaver—not the hunky pinup—Jim is closing in as the students watch, showing the little hammer, touching with his probe the drum itself. Impossibly small. We see the push-me/pull-me of it, the automatic movement that once carried music, small talk, big news.

In lecture we hear about various ear pathologies, including creatures lodged there—the ear mite, the ear ant. Is there an ear bee? asks the most diligent member of the class, surprising us, trading his seriousness for a comic moment. I mean, he adds, making honey from all that wax?

Very funny, says Walker with his slow smile.

11/20   *Life Drawing*

The day to dread. The self-portrait. Grace Benedict warned us. There will be mirrors when you come, she said. I hope for too few so I can gallantly give up mine.

This scheme works at first. I partially set up, then give it away to the sweet tall guy who plays with his band at a local pub. Now and then his classmates go to his gigs, and praise-shower him later. He basks in their words, thanks them for coming.

Unfortunately, Grace finds me a mirror, and I burrow away in the corner. I go for color again, vast sweeps of the pastel whose dust suddenly seems toxic, making me breathe funny. I draw myself. And then color up my face—a regular Dorian Gray. *Go Ugly Early* says a T-shirt blithely sold in a popular bar near campus, the idea abominable and sexist and directed to guys out carousing: find any woman you can right off, to be certain to have someone to take home at the end of the night. But here it is a useful mantra for this self-absorbed exercise.

Because I watch the young women in class tremendously burdened, trying to draw themselves beautiful, seriously alluring. Such suffering. But to give up on that beauty right off—that's freeing!

Grace, as usual, hits the mark: I see you're hiding. So how about a series of smaller drawings, so yes, you can hide in each one, but you end up drawing every part of the face?

Fair enough, I say. But *busted,* I think.

So there are three more "orgy of color" drawings I manage, each looking not anything like the others, each *not* pretty, not pretty at all. A relief.

The totally endearing Asian exchange student who knows very little English stops at my spot in the corner. He looks for a while, turns, sings out with great cheer *Like Matisse!*—pronouncing the *e* at the end as a syllable unto itself, a long flourish.

Like Munch! he says then, doing *The Scream* with his hands clutching the sides of his face.

Matisse and Munch. Light and dark. I like that combo, I tell him. Thank you! He smiles at me.

A long morning staring into the mirror. And yes, that scream.

I figured this would be the day, the one that I've been dreading ever since we unwrapped the heads, the beautiful heads. All this week, however lopped-off their skulls, whatever digging inside required to unveil eye or ear, this day, the worst. What Jim Walker warned: they will lose their faces.

First the lecture, a matter of endless connects and reconnects, nerves and vessels. (The state boards, says Walker, might be heavy on innervation and blood supply, who knows.) And muscles, under the thin skin of the face, so many, at all angles. Hence: expression. Hence the *look* one gives that reveals everything—or hides it. But I want to keep those lovely faces intact. This, the hardest lab, to—say it—*skin* the faces.

Skin: a verb this time, not a noun. *To disfigure,* says David—the real meaning of that word.

In the women's john as we change into our scrubs and lab coats, I hear them talking as usual. So many exams now. So many *freaking out.* And one recalls undergrad exam week—just two years ago, she and her roommate celebrating a break in their grueling study routine.

Popcorn for dinner! she says, because we went to the movies. Sweatpants and T-shirts. And stepped up to order the biggest cartons. The high school girl at the snack counter: *Ladies, really?!* It's her funny critique they savored.

Oh, and then ice cream for dessert! she adds fondly.

We enter the lab where half the cadavers are already released from their plastic and shroud. The dear faces again, unchanged from yesterday, the day before, and before and before. Still up on their blocks—neck block and shoulder block.

The nonhunk, regular-guy group is at it, the skinning. One cheek is gone, down to the lip, into the chin, part of the skin of the nose.

See, a student tells me with such enthusiasm, the temporal artery! It's right next to the ear. A reason we hear our heart pounding at night, I think I recall Jim saying in lecture. On every table lies a top of skull, upright, crushed wet towels inside.

They continue skinning, all of them now, every face. How against that darkened skin, the fact of those faces receding. Ghosting themselves. They keep a rim of mouth, the dark of nostril, the eye and its closed lid. These human spots in the suddenly whitened face. How stripping the face reduces them to the same face, almost.

The students are to isolate the many facial muscles that enable shows of amusement, sorrow, despair, disbelief, joy, hilarity, anger, spite—all those inward states. I see the parotid gland—which makes saliva—back near the ear above the jaw.

For the first time this term, I'm thinking *skeleton*. As before, I am thinking *past life*. But mine too, those previous sweet faces only in my own head now. And it's *metaphor* that distances and saves me. We're *shaving* the face, I tell anyone who will listen. Or they're just negatives of themselves now, I say, like drugstores used to give you along with the real photo for some future redo. I'm struck, undone really: metaphor, this ancient trick and device of poets, goes deep, beyond mere clever decoration. It can heal, is medicinal, I tell myself. It makes the strange into the familiar. It makes what is most terrible almost *bearable*.

The only one with her eyes open—the 100-year-old—now has closed lids. I push them open—the only human thing left in her face—the small delicate blue irises, the watery whites. Somewhere beneath there's the optic nerve in its canal, still leading down to a brain no longer there but across the room floating in its small sea of alcohol and water.

I keep thinking of that temporal artery, just under the skin of each cheek. And John Keats's work on it in surgery—however successful he was that day—convincing him *never again*. To cut the living flesh: violence for a reason. But the act turning him fully to poetry.

11/24   *Cadaver Lab*

The faces are still here, but not as before, of course. I strain to find what I loved in the bone structure, the tissue of muscle and fat, web of nerves and vessels, bits surviving the lancet. When I *do* see that, it's calming.

The 100-year-old still gapes in amazement or bewilderment or distress. The regular guy seems to float, his rim of mouth intact, set, above the fray. In fact they *are* individuals, still themselves. Especially so the nail-polish lady because the students have skinned (hard even to *write* that word) only half her face. So she's an image now, one of those classic textbook pictures to show a *before* and an *after.* Or a favorite of artists in every era—artists with a morbid streak, that is, who want to show half the living face, half the drop down into what's underneath.

Nevertheless I cling to that half of her that gives me her face back, her small delicate features. Again, the unsettling *pink* she is against the gradually beautiful darkening others.

What's particularly recognizable: the rest keep their eyelids and lashes, their lip rim of mouth, points of nose. All keep the flaps of scalp, now lying back where they came from over the lost top of skull, buoyed by the crumpled wet paper towels inside. Mostly the flaps just lie there. But for the big guy, silver pins are inserted to keep them joined. Long silver pins, the sort used for marking certain areas when these students are tested, asked to identify important nerves, joints, muscles, vessels.

I swear their hair is growing—though Walker says no, not possible. The gray stubble on their scalp flaps seems longer. The two men's beards more of a shadow. A moving touch, a human touch, this hair. I run my hand through what's left on the scalp of the 100-year-old to solace myself.

They're working on the neck now. Three triangles there (anterior, posterior, and one smaller area—is it to the side?). I've lost focus, Jim's lecture a great winding wheel of terms and connections on which I almost ride, almost float, to little use. I understand the classmates of John Keats now, their claiming he rarely paid much attention. "Water off a duck's back," they laughed.

I'm that duck too. A living cliché. Quack.

But some bits still stir in me. I come upon someone whose probe pulls up the big fat internal carotid artery, the one that alarms at night, pulsing its steady syncopation as the temporal artery does.

Turn the head, advises our teacher. But in lab this is harder than it sounds. Some of these four—the big guy, of course—have vast perfect places to enter and dissect. The women particularly are difficult.

Odd things: one called the nucleus ambiguus—a spot in the medulla that has controlling links to the heart, the larynx. Or Meckel's cave— that depression inside the bony skull, the bowl, the calvarium, is the top of the skull we hold in our hands. (And who the hell is Meckel anyway?)

Looming above the 100-year-old, one of the young women picks at the many nerves with her probe. I've checked out, she says. I'm not here. It's Thanksgiving! I don't even care about the test this afternoon.

I notice that at the table of the regular-guy cadaver, four scissor-like instruments—hemostats—hanging off the back hem of a student's lab coat. He's intent on his dissection but finally looks back and down. They are softly jingling, swaying. A gag gift, a kind of recognition, if not praise, that his fellow students kept walking by quietly attaching these without his knowledge.

He absorbs this stunt, looks over to several people trying not to laugh at the next table where we're circling the 100-year-old. And grins. Okay guys, he says. They're mine now. You're *not* getting them back!

The students continue removing fat, trying to expose, then get past the so-called strap muscles in the neck—long thick expanses that support and turn the head in all directions.

In lecture, much talk—explanations—about putting dye in nerves, in various vessels, to reveal their sometimes screwy pathways, how they hitchhike with other nerves for a while, then branch off on their own. A metaphor for artistic development, that's sure. Or empathy.

Dye your sorrow. And where does it go, what does it touch?

At the end of lab, Samar says goodbye to me. I won't be back until next term, she says. I'm puzzled but she is smiling.

I'm going on a _____ , she tells me. A word I can't quite parse. Arabia, she adds. Then I hear *Mecca* but not how I usually hear it.

Oh, a *pilgrimage,* I say, suddenly clear that she meant the *haj.* That's fantastic! I tell her. And beaming, she answers all my questions, e.g., What will it be like? The places to stay? What to wear? To eat? A big party? A sacred retreat?

Yes! she says. A once-in-a-lifetime journey.

She will go with her husband, their boys left behind with friends. An epic passage. Her face—underscored and framed by her headscarf—is beautiful.

A moment of pure radiant spirit in this most bodily place.

The endless detail continues in lecture. The screen lights up. Nerves and blood vessels down into the neck. A glut. I drift in and out in the room's half dark.

In lab, they're at it, but I can tell it's the end of the term. So many seem exhausted, pulling more pranks on each other—the hemostat trick earlier, multiplied. Virtually everyone eventually finds such a tail on his or her lab coat. I mention this to another of my favorites, the tough, cool one.

Does this mean you're fair game? she says.

Hey, I say. I'm a stranger in a strange land here.

Meanwhile I've made peace with the beloved faces, have trained myself to *see* them again, how what's left can suggest to almost suffice. The nonhunk regular guy's half a nose, rim of lip, and part of his left cheek still intact under his eye. And the eyelid, his many lashes. They've rubber-banded the flaps of his scalp *back,* but the skinned expanse of his face sharpens it, gives it edge. He's more striking, more dignified somehow.

I see this now, how their faces in the process have become ancient, those of mummies or those first bog people I took them for, holding on for eight thousand years. The eyelids, still closed over each eye. The bone structure that defines each face still evident, no longer just a trace underneath. As before, the nail-polish lady is half and half—half here, half down to the quick, before and after, Earth and whatever's to come, even if it's a glorious nothing.

I learn: the Adam's apple, merely the front edge of the thyroid cartilage. I hear the sound of the handsaw on the clavicle. When that fails, the pierce and thud of chisel and hammer. Now they've draped a towel over the 100-year-old's face.

That's a kindness, I say. She can't see us now.

I did that, says one of the young men. I'm the kind one. And he laughs.
Oh, that evil laugh, I say. And everyone smiles.

Tools, from the labels on the cabinet drawers:

Forceps	Hammers Chisels
Probes	Virchow Skull Breakers
Scissors	Bone Cutters
Power Saws Dremels	Surgical Gloves Masks Sharps
Test Pins	Hemostats
Blade Removers Rope	Handsaws
First Aid Kit	Crossing Saws
OCS Anatomy Saw	Artificial Replacement Models

As I write notes, a partial skull lies beside me on a table. You using that
skull? someone asks.

Funny you should mention that, I say, and pause. Of course I am! Then
pause. Nope. Not really.

He takes it away but is back immediately. Wrong skull, he says.

Earlier, at the end of lecture, one of the students gives his presentation
on new ways to fix a cloudy eye. The former English major in him
makes it clear, entertaining, interesting. To finish, he beams a picture of
a lovely young woman on the screen.

Extra credit, he says, if you can say who this is. Everyone is perplexed.
She's holding a cat.

He beams up a second picture. This time, he's standing behind her, his
arms around her. Both are grinning madly. Same cat.

This is _____ . My fiancée! Everyone applauds. We just announced, he tells us happily.

But does the cat approve? I sing out from the back of the room.

12/2   *Life Drawing*

We're back to the body—someone else's—*not* self-portraits. Then I ask the student next to me—since I missed the last class—what's up? Meaning which paper, which approach, what tools required this time. What are we doing today?

Drawing, he shrugs. And gives me a wry look.

Turns out it's my favorite drill. Fast poses, 20 seconds, several on a page. Welcome back, Matisse! I love doing this. A kind of warm-up. Eventually we end with 40-minute drawings, two of them. One "passive," one "aggressive," meaning color choices, the kind of stroke with pencil or chalk (calm, I guess, or violent).

Too much, too busy. Less is more, for me at least. My *more* is just a mess. It's depressing.

Grace Benedict talks of *intent,* when going in. But I ache for the discovered thing.

12/4   *Life Drawing*

An odd project today. A young woman poses for us. She's been here once or twice before. Self-assured, an amused clarity about her. She doesn't leave her post even for breaks. Ultracalm, just sitting there, speaking to no one, at ease doing nothing. I'm reminded of my sister-in-law, asked by my brother once when he returned home from work a few

weeks after the birth of their first child, *What have you been doing all day?* After a bit of thought, she said, *Making milk!*

Our teacher has us block the big paper in squares. Or at least divide it, top half, bottom half. And draw one part of the figure, then draw it again, same part of the body, in some other way. On the other side of these drawings, we're to focus on another part of her or a very different view of the same part. A little confusing but Grace has examples: large zooming in of head or hand, and sometimes the added bit later crosses that part of the figure, behind it, a strange repetitive dreamlike effect.

You just aren't *creative,* boom! like that, she tells us. You must learn to be.

She's all about intent. Intent: a thing I never trust, what I can't wait to see fall away, flower into another way, a secret passage that surprises.

I begin to draw, mostly with the charcoal pencil. A head, an arm. The model's holding her head. Side view. I complain to Grace how my shading on the figure—shadows cast by the lighting in this room—looks stupid, fake, merely smudgy.

That's because you have no patience, she says. It's tiny little lines you need, and a lot of looking.

(*Keep looking!*—that mantra over and over.)

So I move to another part of the room, to draw her from the other side, same angle of arm, same profile. Now what? I stare and stare. Then go back into the lower-right square with violet this time, and draw the figure starting at chin and throat, to waist, the arm extended and crooked under the penciled figure. Ditto up top. On the left, one I return to from my original spot in the room. Color! And the sweep of the chalk. It's addictive, and I find the shadows so much earlier now.

I love this, I say as Grace circles by.

12/5 *Cadaver Lab*

We're still on the neck, on development of head and neck in the womb, off the gut tube, the nerves and muscle in the tongue, throat, soft palate, hard palate, the tubes going to stomach and lungs.

An ENT guy is visiting, laments that this med school has never produced an ear, nose, throat doc, in spite of the fact that of all office visits, 85 percent are ENT related. He's methodical and sweet, very measured. Does an exam on a class volunteer, who's fine. Various tests, especially on the cranial nerves controlling the automatic and sympathetic moves in the face. The face doctor, really an under-the-face doctor.

In lab, it's the worst day possible. We take off the heads.

How to remove the head, Walker says, as he explains the cuts from the back of the skull first, the fingers slipping in to lift off at C1 or C2, either axis or atlas but only the front goes. Leave the back intact, he says. Apparently if you hit that space right, it just comes off.

I see the work that was done on Wednesday, the day I missed. On every cadaver, the jawbone is exposed—the shock of it now, below the cheek. The smaller second take when I see how the red rubber band holding the 100-year-old's scalp flap together has bled pink in a circle around the cut edge of her skull.

Smoke now, that terrible bone smell once more. One can see small swirls of smoke again in the bright light. I'm holding my hand over my nose. Someone offers me a surgical mask—so thoughtful, because this helps as I hold it up to my face. She and another young woman follow suit. It *is* terrible, this smell. And it stays in the nasal passages a long time. The sound too—that electric saw. Relentless. Indifferent.

Hard work. The skull seems impossible to cut. But soon the back third is released and pieces taken out. The trick is somehow to take off the remaining head. A young woman with the electric saw, handsaw, and then—yes, Dr. Walker was right—the chisel, the hammer. She pounds at the vertebrae and the head thrusts forward, but nothing is released.

We have to lift her up, one of them says about the 100-year-old. And there are thick triangular long blocks for that, several people at once lifting her, a medical team at bedside, careful, such a human response to help a patient upright to sit and—what?—take food, take medicine? The sorrowful, touching irony of such a gesture here in the cadaver lab.

They work, two of the students holding her shoulders, one chiseling, then twisting her neck, his hands on what remains of her skull. I think of Brigit's poem about the killing of the goat and its decapitation: *it was harder work than they had imagined.*

Because: the head doesn't want to leave the body. It simply doesn't. This seems to me the hardest *parting* they've done. Everyone is anxious, working somewhere between frantic and *careful,* every little move. Such strength is involved, real muscle since the angle is all wrong. Medicine: such a communal effort. But the young woman there from the start with the saw, she steps up again.

I'm standing with the sweet wry one next to all this. He suddenly says to me: Sometimes during this semester, I think you have to step out and see what we're doing as an outsider might see it.

He pauses. This is one of those times, he says.

12/8   *Cadaver Lab*

So the heads are off in cadaver lab. This is the day to split the head in half, our teacher tells us, beginning his lecture on the nose, the vast empty space the nasal passages take up in the skull, the sinuses attached to that, the now-and-then slide down to the throat, the mouth. I learn a perfectly reasonable but surprising fact: to clear the sinuses, just tilt your head to the side for a while. Then tilt the other way. Then forward. The hardest sinus cleaning requires that you stand on your head. Either that or lie on a bed, head hanging over the side. Which is to say, gravity is our friend—the housecleaner of those vast inner spaces, how to empty them.

But it's totally unnerving in lab, the heads fully removed, just lying on the tables apart, horrific because of that, the image back to prehistory, beginning then but current, internet-current. How small the face is now, how the head just lies there on its side.

Again the saws come out. Handsaws exclusively this time because the cuts must be more delicate. Again the smoke and the scent of bone dust, and the sound. It's hard work, and hard to look *at,* these young women and men sawing down the face. Impossible, almost, to write about this.

Two of the four students in each group work on their half, finding the nasal passages, the major nerves and arteries as usual. One surprise in cutting the fingernail lady—her group hits plastic. They cry out: her false teeth!

That's not supposed to happen, someone says to me. They take them out before the embalming. Or they should have.

They haven't. I see the split uppers, the intact lowers, a full set, on the metal table now as the group works on that dear face.

One amazing fact is the clear rungs in the large nasal passage, called *conchae,* like a shell. Their purpose: to humidify the air that comes in as it drops through those rungs. The body seems to think of most everything—except how finally *not* to die.

Amazing personal fact: those hemostats clipped on people's lab coats as a joke, a prank? I feel something weighted down there . . .

I've been hemostated! I look across the lab to one of the groups, laughing. And they *are* laughing. That's it. I've arrived! Targeted. I've passed! Chosen.

12/9   *Life Drawing*

I'm late, get there right after the 10:00 break, knock, and am admitted. My oldest friend, Palmira Brummett, visiting family in Chicago, was here overnight, and there was coffee and breakfast and a chat before she got on the road back to Knoxville, where she teaches history.

We talked partly of *heads,* the long grisly tradition in all cultures, of war, of where, and her special fascination: their iconography on maps. In her new book from Cambridge, a whole chapter on heads, she tells me.

In class, our model is the large ample older woman I haven't seen since the start of the term. She's lying on her side now; above her on the high edge of the couch, the skeleton laid out in the same position. Maybe Grace Benedict's black humor revealed! But everyone is earnest, as usual.

I set up as quietly as possible, being the truant, the latecomer. It occurs to me how like Quaker meetings these sessions are—Quaker meetings, where no one's rushing to say anything. But Grace and I have discussed this with joy more than once: don't you love the sound here? The scratching, rubbing, people furiously drawing. Yes. And such a *yes* in that sound.

I manage two drawings on my good paper. The first I lay down in charcoal pencil, then use blue pastel. For the second, I go straight for pastel, violet this time, and skip the underdrawing. A nervy and thrilling thing to do.

The skeleton—I've forgotten it and must add it at the end, in miniature, in the left-hand high corner. Life/death. A fitting combination, here at the end of my term. But haunting me from the first.

12/10 Final Day in Cadaver Lab

A lecture—and dissection—completely on the larynx. Which means in lecture the truly fascinating and accessible facts of the voice box and vocal cords. And most amazing, Jim Walker's videos of various surgeries to correct speech (mainly hoarseness), removal of cysts and polyps, cancers, and the repair of lesions. With a soundtrack, before-and-after audio bits of patients reciting the Goldilocks story (*And Mama Bear, Father Bear says . . .*) to bring home the difference.

We change clothes and enter the lab for the last time. I have to say the cadavers really are disturbing now, picked over, in ruins, the heads still split, of course, hardly recognizable anymore unless my eye lands on an eye, a stray eye. The 100-year-old's a watery blue, sunken a bit, as if dreaming somewhere in the still-there.

A crucial fact: is the larynx attached to the head or the body at this point? I think the head. But no, it must be the body since the removal was at C1 or C2. Either way, I see the vocal cords themselves. Tiny. And two kinds, false and true, the former encircling the latter. So neatly engineered, given a double tubing—for food and breath—how the way in and down the throat is still separate, the flaps that close and open to keep the passages not in use quite sealed. I see those too, both in the nifty plastic model passed around and in the bodies themselves.

I think this: all those words said in love or indifference, the endlessly usual passage of song or talk, at least in this foursome, their so many long years. The welling up of life behind this silence.

12/11   *Last Drawing Class*

I should be doing the one final-exam drawing—"showing your strengths." But I do two—one I drop halfway through, it's so awful (charcoal pencil, NuPastels). The model is a guy we've had a lot; terrific at this, never moving.

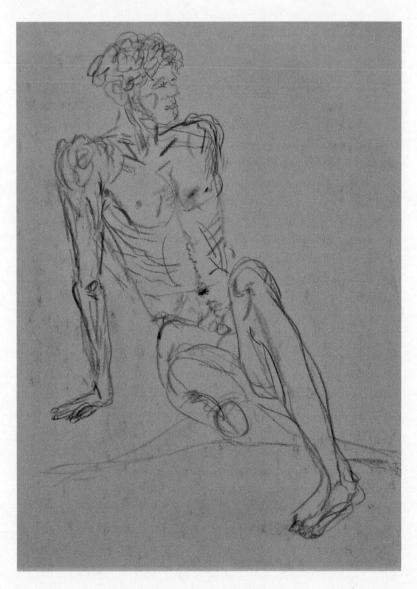

My second—a close-up—head, upper body only. Charcoal, and I'm more careful, trying to *get it,* the shading. Which I do not. It's terrible too. I miss what I easily do—the flashing, quick, reckless sort of drawing. But I've discovered colored pencil, Grace's favorite.

I allow myself a little color then, a few pastels, as backdrop.

12/12 I Jìng Zhòng *My Teachers*

So Jim Walker, Grace Benedict, and I go to lunch. (Samar would have too, if she hadn't gone off for her trip of a lifetime.) Grateful, I want to treat them, and it dawns on me to ask whether they want to do this together. They seem excited to meet each other. So I make reservations at Bistro 501, high-toned, perhaps for all of us but certainly a rare visit to that place for me.

I offer Jim a ride, which he readily takes. Grace meets us there.

Great connections, a large *who knew?* between those two—Grace from that part of Canada directly above Michigan, where Jim was raised. They were virtually neighbors and knew all the same beautiful spots as children. We talk teaching, talk bodies, talk a whole rich range of things through beers and salmon and salad and chocolate mousse. Three hours, until we are the last ones in the joint. They close at two, but with their permission, we hang on undisturbed as they tidy up around us. We talk about students until Grace excuses herself, and Jim and I drive back to Purdue.

One funny note: when I entered the place with Jim Walker, before Grace arrived, Cindy MacDonald—neighbor, fellow mother of a high school music student—was having lunch with a few friends. I had told her something about the cadaver lab months ago, egged on by her amused curiosity.

So how did that med school class turn out? she sings out as we walk by. The one with the bodies? The cadavers?—her voice in a dramatic stage whisper. Her lunch mates are startled. *Cadavers?!*

I explain how I am "taking my teacher to lunch"—in fact, this very one, from that very class. I point to Jim, who looks both sheepish and surprised, suddenly a celebrity!

In all, a terrific end. I'm glad I could honor them, *"jing zhòng"* them— as our Chinese students used to say when David and I taught in Taiwan, way back in the late '70s, early '80s.

Toward the end of the lunch, Jim pipes up: You know, this is really great. I *never* hang out with anyone outside of the School of Science!

III

The Fossil Record

Fall 2008　The UK in Fragments

London

The Hunterian Museum

Ovaries of a Surinam toad, of a newt, a monkfish, a salamander, a grass snake, a viper, a young torpedo ray, a spotted dogfish.

The barber surgeons. Bodies for dissection—executed criminals. Dissected bodies exhibited around the hall. Barber pole: the reminder of the barber surgeons. Bloody bandaged arm out front.

Small models of human bodies in ivory, with movable internal organs, used to explain to patients their pain, discomfort, etc. without the need of examination.

John Hunter, teacher of Keats: A surgeon "is like an armed savage who attempts to get that by force which a civilized man would get by stratagem" (from his *Lectures on the Principles of Surgery*).

"Every tool has two ends, one working on the matter, the other on the man."—John Halsham, *Lonewood Corner,* 1907.

The Old Operating Theatre Museum and Herbarium

Hildegard of Bingen (!)—her guide to herbal remedies (*Liber simplicis medicinae*). "St. Kessog martyred, his body was returned to Luss, wrapped in herbs to preserve it."

Types of poultices—linseed oil for burns, sage and vinegar for bruises and sprains, comfrey for deep cuts and broken bones or for drawing foreign bodies out, onion for lung congestion, mustard for chest colds, resin for supporting joints, belladonna for back pains.

A Book of Simple Drugs—De materia medica of Dioscorides. Greek, translated into Arabic, 1334.

The British Museum

Nicobar Islands, the Bay of Bengal: Spirits are associated with the forests, the open sea, the dead. Most dangerous: people who died violently or away from home. If a sick person doesn't respond to herbal meds, the problem is a malignant spirit. A doctor/priest is brought in to dispel it.

Egyptian mummy wrappings: "gave the corpse the appearance of a transfigured being."

Mummification: the head and limbs were wrapped first. Layers of cloth soaked in resin, packing of mud and earth between to make the "required shape" of the mummy. Amulets were placed in among the wrapping. A rolled funeral papyrus was sometimes placed between the legs.

A huge leap from the Egyptian canopic jars to "bucket of spinal cords" and the use of plastic bags to store organs in the cadaver lab. Carved

heads on those jars: a man for Imsety, a baboon for Hapy, a jackal for
Duamutef, a falcon for Qebehsenuef.

Egyptian *The Book of Two Ways,* written between 2000 and 1600 BCE,
a guide to the afterlife, two paths, water and earth. Main task: to join
the sun god Ra.

More canopic vases—used for organs: brain, lungs, stomach, liver.
Various gods painted there—dog head, hawk head, man head, baboon
head. And stuff there too—bracelets, charms, necklaces, amulets
of precious stones. Scarabs plugged in the heart with an apology
(chapter 30, *The Book of the Dead*).

Babylonians—foretold the future by reading the blemishes on the
entrails (liver, intestines) of animals. Don't we do that in cadaver lab,
but in reverse? Not to know the future, but to figure the body's failures
in the past?

A thread cross is a device used when appropriate mantras are recited,
can capture either beneficial or evil forces. Some traps placed on the
roof to ensnare demonic spirits.

Sirens, female-headed birds, hold smaller figures, which may be souls of
the deceased. "Harpy Tomb"—after the four female-headed birds at the
corners.

EDINBURGH

Surgeons' Hall

The right hand with an eye in the palm is a symbol of the "healing hand"
associated with medicine. "The hand that sees"—a reference to the
surgeon's hand working as if it had sight, inside the human body.

"Try to learn the features of a disease or injury as precisely as you know the features, the gait, the tricks of manner of your most intimate friend. Him, even in a crowd, you can recognize at once."—Joseph Bell, Royal College of Surgeons of Edinburgh, who taught Arthur Conan Doyle.

Thick glass jars of femur, tibia, cervical axis, radius, ulna, humerus, the spine of a child with tuberculosis.

Wounds to the heart: fork, knife, gunshot.

In medieval Europe, the correct way to let blood was judged by a study of the heavenly constellations and the moon, a practice still beloved in the Renaissance.

Bloodletting, from Hippocrates (c. 460–375 BCE), who claimed health was a state of active/passive balance of body fluids to be called *humus*— bile and phlegm, most importantly, blood and black bile. The Romans said these were associated with the four elements from which the world was formed: air, water, fire, ash.

    Excess of phlegm obvious in the cold of winter.

    Excess of bile during summer's diarrheal periods.

    Excess of melancholy, dreaming due to excess of black bile.

For real, in real time, I walk past a girl with a broken right hand in a partial cast seated on the floor, drawing a skull with her left hand, clearly the wrong one.

Spring 2009   Italy in Fragments

NORTHERN ITALY

Remember: The shrine made by the gardeners at Bellagio. That Susan and I drew it. That Rodney and Elizabeth put flowers there.

Pliny the Younger got here first, that first villa on the site named Tragedy. Below, on the shores of Lake Como, his other villa, named Comedy.

The Memoriale della Shoah, Milan

"The Mourned"—starting with the 14th century, medieval sculpture moved beyond the crucified Christ and virgin with child. Others say "the mourned" is a sacred repetition of the moment following the deposition of the cross and preceding the entombment: the pious women, weeping. But it's a habit, an entry, a category for art historians.

The gratuitous persistent breast exposed (one) in one of the mourners at the foot of the cross.

Night train from Milano to Roma—the ladder, the little elastic woven bag on the wall for eyeglasses, etc., the little cup holders, the tiny fold-down shelf, the blue comforter, cotton sheets and pillowcases, the table below that transforms to a sink, the now-and-then presence of the threatening world outside, someone trying the locked door all night, a sudden secretive noise.

Light and dark, what's left behind, memory, disappearance, composure in pain, history of silence and secret, brains in jars, catacombs, the train all night.

Rome

Trajan's Column

At the base, battle garments in array, tunics, chain-mail shirts, helmets, etc. No bodies except the *form* of the chest in such garments lies beneath shields, spears. Very spooky. Then: like David's grandmother's memory did it when 103 years old, all are staged as simultaneous events, same size from the ground up. Which means they must enlarge, be carved bigger as the eye moves higher and higher on the column.

Keats's House

The little garden out on the back fire-escape-looking porch (the Spanish Steps so close!); not violets or daisies but white rose and some blue flower I can't place.

Off the body of John Keats once, the plaster death mask of the face survives but not the two casts made of his hand and his foot, also a practice of the day. Vanished, probably crushed to dust. Or someone made off with them.

"How long will this posthumous life of mine last?" His demand. Every day.

Vatican law required they burn everything in the room in which the poet died, even the wallpaper, linens, bed, carpet . . . thinking TB passed like the plague.

Roman doctor, 2 CE, described one of his tuberculosis patients as having "shoulder blades like the wings of birds." TB—known as *phthisis*—Greek for "wasting."

Fanny B's unopened and unread love letters to Keats—buried with him.

"In the 19th century, it was common for friends to exchange locks of hair as tokens of affection. After death, these became precious keepsakes, or if from a famous head, prized relics."

Leigh Hunt, introducing Keats in *The Examiner*, 1816: "In fact it is wrong to call it a new school, . . . it's only object being to restore the same love of Nature, and of *thinking* instead of mere *talking*, which formerly rendered us real poets, not merely versifying wits, and bead-rollers of couplets."

Near where Keats is buried in the Protestant Cemetery:

> *Rom*
>
> *Du bist eine Welt*

The Forum

The statues. The way some of the heads are crooked, eyes closed in pain or ecstasy, who can tell. Or in sleep some dream like that, passing through a tunnel of dream to eternity.

Other heads looking down, some sternly or sweetly straight ahead, all with hair that curls uncombed or with a headband slipped on. So many noses gone, and on the torsos, carved six-packs that could sell exercise videos. And the fragile scrotum made of stone now belies its grief that the penis is gone. But the shoulders are draped in the most opulent scarves. *Opulent.* I never wrote that word before.

The puzzle pieces of the frescoes, so many bits missing. Or the carved marble trim, two figures facing each other, arms extended. Or a column overflowing with flowers. So often missing: a belly, a neck, an arm. In

the same room, the shadow, that shade, a black-marble statue, a woman
in long robes who seems to salute the living.

Only one statue has kept its head.

The habit of people in museums to ape the statues, arm raised when
the stone arm is up, head turned the same frozen way. And the cameras
click away.

Suggrundaria: graves of infants under the eaves.

Pratica di Mare, Ficana and Ardea: habit of burying older children on
the edge of family property—a way to claim the estate. Last phase of
that settlement at the Forum—630 to 620 BCE.

To live among the ruins—a 17th-century landscape painting of Rome.
Ancient bits of pillars on their sides at bus stops. Like the body in old
age, like the corpses the center of all traffic in the cadaver lab, the young
here and there just living their lives. And then there are the famous feral
cats of Rome—multiple, extraordinary.

Relics, the most Catholic thing I remember from childhood in the
church, the "disembodied body part" vs. more ancient Roman ideas of
order and wholeness. *Statue of a Seated Philosopher,* 1625—but minus
head, minus hand, minus half a foot anyway. Where are they?

St. Sebastian churns under the arrows that pierce through into axilla
and abdomen, beneath and to the left of the navel. Any excuse to paint
the naked body. Sebastian, in so many canvases! (Even in corners,
foregrounds, backdrops . . .) *Because* he was protector—one of his
many jobs—patron saint of plague survivors as a survivor himself of
his first martyrdom attempt. So the habit then: putting him into the
most unlikely paintings—even a Nativity!—to charm luck, to keep that
deadly virus at bay.

Position of hands in these paintings: Pointing

                                  Accepting

                                  Blessing

                                  Cradling

                                  Holding

                                  Lifting

                                  Grasping

                                  Reaching

                                  Pulling

Everyone in paintings—the artist must decide—looks down or out of the picture. Or straight up, or to the side.

Aesculapius—Roman god of medicine. His staff, that stick with the snake curled around, still with us.

Birds on Roman frescoes: sparrows, ducks, doves, blackbirds, swans, herons, peacocks, robins—"sometimes catching insects or defending themselves against cats."

Also: bands of figured friezes below the *loculi* (funeral niches) depicting still lifes, animals, party scenes, mythological episodes, baskets of cherries and figs, swatches of pomegranates, myrtle, violet. Hercules and the centaur Nessus, pygmies struggling with crates, Prometheus chained to a rock, Apollo and Artemis killing the children of the proud Niobe. Playful figures, leaping, sitting to chat with cupids.

Meanwhile: *bidentalia*—places struck by lightning, considered to be a negative omen by the Romans. Such places when enclosed by a fence and with a stone buried to symbolize the bolt that came down quick.

A sign says: *hippogriffs* ...

A large bronze forearm, from elbow to fingertip. Bigger than a person.

On a large sarcophagus of domestic and vast battle scenes—"the faces of the principal characters remain incomplete, waiting the carving of features of the dead people." Those killed . . .

A sculpture: bent naked figure of a woman. A small hand on her lower back. Nothing else left of the child once attached to it.

The figures are fading on the frescoes, a woman with a jug, a winged horse, a figure—maybe still a woman—is mere shadow. A cliché that is an oxymoron. One arm might be holding up her skirt. Then maybe not.

The Villa of Livia

Livia's garden, on the wall, bluest background. Ilex: a plant used in ominous prophecies. Laurel: sacred to Apollo, symbol of triumph. Box: linked to Hades, god of afterlife. Arbutus: used in funerals, again, to protect the dead. Myrtle: for Pliny, sacred to Aphrodite. Oleander: symbol of death, toxic. Opium poppy: a narcotic. Cabbage rose: love, sacred to Aphrodite.

The Vatican Museums

St. Bartholomew flayed, circa 1500. Eyes closed, gilt pie plate as halo behind his head.

St. Sebastian again, arrows into him all the way to the feathers.

Extreme states showing ecstasy, wonder, shock, pain from torture. All states of being.

Someone always getting propelled into heaven: Christ, Mary, various saints.

St. Sebastian gets tended for his arrow wounds by a beautiful young woman, St. Irene, 1579.

The Sistine Chapel. Famous touch of god and Adam. Two panels away, Adam and Eve—Eve takes the apple from a snake whose head and body resemble a human arm. In fact, the whole upper half of the snake *is* human.

Relics: St. Francis Xavier's arm—hand to elbow in the Jesuit church.

Of all the crucifixion paintings, David says, "That's the deadest dead Christ we've seen." *Really* gray, beat-up body and face. Not the idealized beautiful Christ at all. I look again: head lolling, wounds darkened, greenish skin, figure exhausted from the sacrifice.

St. Peter's Basilica

The *body* of John XXIII under glass at St. Peter's below the giant painting of St. Jerome on his deathbed. John's red embroidered slippers, eyes closed under his red plush beanie. Jerome in gray beard, long hair, looking quite deranged. The pilgrims line up with their earphones for the audio tour. John is very white. A nun sits next to me, quiet at her rosary.

The Borghese Gallery

The Florentine school, 16th century. "Painters distinguished by their formal and chromatic delicateness as well as the serenely contemplative tone that succeeds in making even the scene of martyrdom into an image of absolute composure."

The Bernini sculptures. Stone looks so soft—how does he do this? Pluto grasps Proserpina's thigh, the marble gives and droops exactly like life. *Ratto di Proserpina,* two tears on her cheek. Cerberus: the three-headed dog. Apollo and Daphne = transformation. Woman to tree. Each side completely and self-contained as *other* but the progression so clear.

A 10-foot panel of a crowd of Romans, faces rubbed almost featureless, half the shoulders gone, two legs for all of them still intact, all looking to the right, pretty much in profile.

Dormitorium (Latin) and *koimētērion* (Greek) for cemetery: to sleep, *sleeping place,* for the transfer of lives.

***

Possible poems:

—a few might circle what it is to draw in Keats's death room. Drawing the drawing by Severn, drawing the fireplace irons, the death mask, then to watercolor, i.e., to dream ... cadaver thinking about the inside of her coffin and what she'd put there.

—muscle nerve blood bone heart: thoughts toward the shape of the possible book of poems I hope to write. A section on hand, arm, leg, head. Or a first section laid down among saints, transformations, language of medicine, Keats somehow. And the second? If only the cadavers could speak.

—relics, the Catholic thing, "the disembodied body part" vs. Roman/ pagan ideas.

—the coin's *tink* in the battered metal box to relight the Caravaggios in the vast church. One looks first at the head, the brilliant darkened faces.

—the idea of a cabinet of wonders. A place to put treasures.

—a meditation on the shapes of bones—the skinny moon of ribs, the heart of sacrum, shovel of pelvis and shoulder blade, knuckle of ...

"I should like to paint portraits which would appear after a century to the people living then as apparitions."—Vincent van Gogh to brother Theo, 1888.

"I want to paint men and women with something of the eternal which the halo used to symbolize."—Again, Vincent to Theo.

Then his "In either figure or landscape, I should wish to express not sentimental melancholy but serious sorrow."—Ditto. Ditto. Ditto.

Fossil: bones in stone rot but leave a space.

IV

First Trespass

—In which

      what happened, happens again. One so-be-it *whoosh.* The usual
suspect as speaker, the fortunate one, lost and darkened in the cloud
and the privilege, those weeks and weeks.

—In which

      their voices take over: the cadaver speaks, the 100-year-old,
my favorite. She's small. I touch her shoulder and my hand
stays there. And the 70-year-old, the cadaver pinup, I called him: huge,
   all muscle, every organ and vessel intact,
                          astonishing. Or my
fellow student in the drawing class who knew so little English,
who put his hands on each side of his face, whispering
Munch! when he saw my terrible self-portrait.

—In which

      Yes, my drawing teacher said: *look, think, make a mark.*
                                     Look,
I told myself, and waited to be marked.

—In which

       Yes, over the four cadavers, first day and every day, my anatomy
           teacher,
his mantra: Identify, Appreciate. Move on.
                             (And if I can't move on? or she can't
or he can't or any of us, or all of us . . .)

—In which

       drawing is *thing,* is *creature.* Its doing multiplies,
    divides for gesture, blind contour, straight lines, curves,
           pen and ink, charcoal; pastels, dazzling
       addiction to color,
the awful self-portraits—forgive me.

—In which

       Leonardo is drawing. Or Michelangelo. As long as their notebooks
lie closed or opened in this place or that place, they
                         keep drawing. Because the figures
speak, the partial, unfinished ones,
those abandoned by accident or because a stroke of red chalk fell
all wrong.

—In which

       of course the body's triumphant and ruined before
anything happens on those tables:
                       lung and heart, spleen and spinal cord,
passage of nerve and blood just
below the brilliant yellow sub-cu or buried deeper, in muscle, layer

and layer thereof. The flashing silver is
probe, is scalpel. The tiny handheld saw screams
quietly to ribs and skull, smoke rancid and lazy, snaking up
the light in that place.

—In which

       I draw in class, twice a week, for half the day. How
to *mean* with no words? Private the room
and the windows shaded, private those of us
banished to our paper and our charcoal,

                              the *tic-tic* of that,
private the figure who strips down
who becomes no one this hour.

—In which

       Samar, our other teacher, disappears in December.
It's once a life, this going to Mecca. A *pilgrimage,* she seriously, happily
   tells me
though I mishear in the lab under the racket
of breaking and entering and exhaustion, her jubilant word morphing to—
mirage, I keep hearing. Any voyage, I think. Especially here,
the figure going imaginary . . .

—In which

       Keats closes his *London Dissector,* then opens it, then closes it.
Guy's Hospital, as usual, *o lucky guy,* best place in England to train. Cadavers,
a stack of them pinched from the graveyard last night.

                                  Hear them?
The *resurrection* men who rob the graves deliver
      half-drunk, before dawn.

—In which

Keats enters this? How dare you. Let him rest. Let them all rest,
for chrissake.

—In which

at the lab's side table, anyone could count as calmly as I did:

1) a vial of tiny ear machinery—incus and malleus and stapes,
2) one plastic tub marked *spinal cords,*
3) four brains afloat in their buckets—for next semester, my teacher says.

—In which

the scent of the lab follows me to my car or up the stairs.
One of the med students: Oh   my   god.   I'm at a party?
And suddenly I smell *cadaver* on me!

—In which

the faces, finally unshrouded in November, heads
in wet towels since August.
First words: stunned (*I'm* stunned), beautiful (*they're* beautiful)
as if the finest charcoal pencil has done its work,
their eyes closed or not closed, mouths made simple by lines but one's
open, so *about to,* I lean toward her.

—In which

this list within a list, human gestures all the time: *but how to draw
those*

a) at the swimming pool, in or out of water
b) at Pay Less or Marsh, down an aisle lined with oranges
c) at any corner—specifics!—but who wouldn't walk against
   the light, a street that empty?

Or you draw by x-ray, past clothes, skin, near where tendon threads each bone.
Inside out: another way to imagine, in your miner's helmet and ash.

—In which

so crucial the model in drawing class
means—we take turns when he oversleeps and doesn't show.
                         Me, my turn
on the platform, sinking deeper into my sweater and jeans.
I close my eyes to fend off
their eyes. The Elgin Marbles at the British Museum, their blanks mean
time wearing off the garish colors the Greeks put there.
                                        What colors?
Like DayGlo, the most official one tells us.
Horrific colors, she says briskly. Such bad taste, she adds.

—In which

Keep looking, says my drawing teacher. Or:
Connect those figures. Do something with the background.

—In which

my mother's nearing death again, never wanting
to open her eyes. Her pretending to sleep—
                         I knew that. Her pretending
not to be there. Not the hospital. Not anywhere anymore.

—In which

      I take the long underground passage to the cadaver lab, early morning
all fall. These are the catacombs, I tell myself. I'm entering the netherworld,
I think and thought for at least three weeks in.
                              O angel of familiarity who
erases all wonder . . .
I was rushing then. I was on time. Or I was late.
The elevator door opened to just a hallway to get through.

—In which

      the chain-mail veil begins
at the base of the ribs, drops down, unsecured at the pelvis,
the *greater omentum,* its glistening golden bits of fat,
                        dizzy wiry turns of—
what is that made of? I ask. Thinking tabernacle.
Thinking: this is where the Catholics, the Jews got their
big idea. The Holy of Holies to protect.
                        What isn't built by metaphor?
First it was crucial: the colon, the intestines transforming
   everything into small-enough-to-matter.

—In which

      at the museum, we see the musket ball
from Gettysburg, still embedded in the femur. We see the skull
         from Waterloo sliced by saber, jagged cuts
in the bony surface still visible.

—In which

    Sherlock Holmes solves his crimes: you diagnose
like a doctor obsessed, who thinks
of nothing else, who makes the leap,
                             2 plus 2 might well equal 5.

—In which

    the body's wired plainly, nerves off
the spinal cord, off that knob and tube of vertebrae. But such
    here to there seems suspect, city built badly on city,
the old house rewired on the cheap though it mainly works.
                         O what a piece of work is man—
More amazing: that these jerry-built circuits spark at all.

—In which

    before all this, *in utero,* it's the simple gut tube, the cardiac tube,
their gradual vast intricate complications to come.
                           Start bland, start general.
We grow strange, grow strange, grow strange.

—In which

    the stillness of the cadaver is nothing
like the stillness of the model in drawing class who longs to move her leg,
her arm, her how-many-minutes-to-the-10-minute-break.

—In which against

        the ponderous, more Latinate *words for,*
the lovely, weirder most ordinary names leap out: the hand's
anatomical snuffbox or those empty spaces, the
                        pouch of Douglas, pouch of Morrison
and the skull's interior, small craters as if someone
entered with a candle to claim *Meckel's cave,* passing on
his bloodless lineage. Little *junior.* O little
named-after-me-me-me.
            The anatomists sweeten their lists.

—In which

        okay, then this too: my mother returns.
Maybe she knows me, the hospital dulling
out color, all sound.
Or my grandmother's demented words once hopelessly
tangled—sewing machine for
                    typewriter, her *where's my ball?* for
false teeth. I hear them too.
      Or my friend June, in her eighties, her memory shot, a rim
of *just heard, just seen*—three hours' worth maybe—circles her
each afternoon. *How was your day?* All that she can
or can't remember. No. No way she can rest.
                       Which is worse,
O Doctor Book-of-Life with your
true and toxic. *How dare you.* Which loss?—that
which really happened *unhappens* or how to *tell* those things?
      Sure. As if the brain and heart could choose.

—In which

      begin again this list, how it hypnotizes
to write over and under hundreds of things
                         I'm forgetting. Or never
knocked to open. From such a distance
each was a dot, each was smoke.
      Write it! wrote Bishop for a reason.

V

Figure   Gone   Imaginary

THE FIGURE

can be traced to prehistory, carefully wedded to cave walls and ceilings by blood, spit, and whatever those ancient artists/shamans extracted from stems, burnt wood, and stone shavings to darken, to make color itself transferable and semi-eternal. An archeologist told me they most likely were women, their smaller hands traced on the walls proof. They fleshed out animal and human figures caught in dream or the hunt as history or prophecy, for bragging rights or prayer. At least to time-stop the drama, to remember via a hard surface, to leave it there and walk away so the day's ordinary business could go on, encouraged, the brain undistracted for a while, unencumbered by memory.

I just mistyped *unencumbered*. My schoolmarm computer flashed up the correction and under it offered its robot-splained alternatives as spellcheck is wont to do. I read my options:

creative

imaginative

tangential

It's the *tangent* buried there that flies. Crosses over. Doesn't know quite where it might go.

GONE

A disclosure: When I first began to write the long poem "Cadaver, Speak" before it had a name, I slipped into the typical third dimension of poet-who-tells-what-it-is-like-to-be-a-poet, the observer of self wherever that full-of-herself might be observing in the world that moment.

Which is to say, I wrote the first two or three sections in that voice, with that eyepiece, i.e., *When they opened* her, *I saw the darkest dark lived in there . . .* Which is now to acknowledge yet another *O me me me, sanctified lucky sucker, the one who saw, who lived to tell the tale!* I was writing those first lines at Bellagio, given a month in that most beautiful 15th-century Italian villa the Rockefeller Foundation has taken from time and history and handed over to artists, writers, scholars, composers to do what they might manage to do.

I read these first bits to my husband, my lifetime beloved, who looked immediately uneasy. Translation: *whose story is this?* Slowly that sank in. Me me me—okay okay—oh god, not again.

In that heavy pause, *she* moved in, she who I had met in the cadaver lab and so upended me. Maybe I began taking dictation, became her Girl Friday. I do understand I was waiting. Suspended. In wait for the real poem, the real spirit, the one who had lived and still did. Outside there were boats; I could hear them on the two famous ancient lakes that joined just below our window. A place of brain-dissolving beauty.

Then: *When* they *open* me, *the darkest dark must live in there . . .* Shift of person, of point of view. Suddenly *she* was speaking. And the 32-sequence poem flooded me with detail from my notes, quoted ordinary talk, wonder, regret, gratitude, rememberings (hers, I swear!) of the 100-year-old we had dissected. I remained a dodgy character in her drama, "the quiet one" whom my cadaver disdained and wrote off. Because. And because I pissed her off.

And what was I anyway? She would be the teller of this tale, *thank you very much*.

Duh. Was I even thinking?

Get real, poet as conduit, blank synapse to be leapt by wiser, richer spirits.

IMAGINARY

I think now that oldest cadaver, her body, was a map, a tracing, evidence of a life that carried weight beyond any poor imagining I might do. I drew from my notes in the lab and from my time in the drawing studio and beyond, places across the sea. I drew urgently from love—my grandmother's same small shape, same blue eyes, those small-town summers I spent with her. But it was the body through time and space, back and back, in sickness and in health, that kept haunting me.

The ancient Norse god of war and magic and poetry, Odin, counted on two ravens. One he called *Thought,* the other *Memory.* These he sent out daily, to reconnoiter and return with whatever vital news, good or bad.

The two ravens I've known came back, however ragged, for this curious book. The shadow of their wings darkens these pages.

Acknowledgments

I need to say straightaway that any medical (and otherwise) misinformation, misremembering, misstatements are completely my fault. *Mea culpa!* But what follows are my genuine thank-yous.

Continuing warmth and gratitude to my colleagues and teachers who with no hesitation welcomed me into their lab and studio, now Emeritus Professor James Walker and Adjunct Professor Samar Khirallah of the IU Medical School on Purdue's campus, and artist Grace Benedict, formerly of the Patti and Rusty Rueff School of Visual and Performing Arts at Purdue.

I thank the Provost's Office at Purdue for the Faculty Fellowship in the Study of a Second Discipline, which gave me the chance to disappear into Life Drawing and the Gross Human Anatomy class that fall, 2008. That fellowship is a brilliant idea that meant much to a lot of people. I hope someday it will be resurrected.

Much appreciation for the artist residency at the American Academy in Rome, and the month's residency at the Rockefeller Foundation's villa at Bellagio, spring 2009, which supported my writing and research.

I thank editor Carolyn Kuebler of the *New England Review,* who took a chance and published "Shards," and thank editors Elizabeth Scanlon of *The American Poetry Review* and Wayne Miller and Jo Luloff of *Copper Nickel,* who likewise published "The Body Floats Regardless" (as "Book One: Notes of Origin" and "Book Two: Notes of Origin," respectively). Meanwhile, the quoted bit on page 10 is John Keats's, from his poem "Ode to a Nightingale," written in 1819 and committed to memory by so many, with good reason.

Of course I am deeply grateful that editor Michael Wiegers of Copper Canyon Press somehow trusted me, publishing in 2014 what came of these notes and drafts—my eighth poetry collection, *Cadaver, Speak*. I'm thankful too for his allowing the early incarnations—ghostly seeds now—of those poems to settle here, in this book. And thank Zeus for stellar editor John Pierce who generously came out of happy retirement to aid and abet in the peculiarities of its making. Also warm gratitude to Jessica Roeder, Claretta Holsey, Ryo Yamaguchi, and Ashley E. Wynter at Copper Canyon Press.

Other people—friends—to thank: Kathy Evans, artist and art librarian at Purdue, who advised me about images used at the end of the book and whose own experience observing in the cadaver lab encouraged me; and Gail Dodge, former physical therapist and Pilates teacher for whom all the mysterious bones and muscles and joints make perfect sense. Thanks also to my fellow students in both classes that now long-ago fall for their good will and good humor, and to compatriots in and out of Purdue's English Department and my MFA students there who kindly kept any misgivings about this semi-mad scheme pretty much to themselves, even after their visit to the lab.

Loving remembrance of poet and friend Brigit Pegeen Kelly, whose crucial advice appears in my journal notes, who never blinked an eye about any of it.

Finally, profound affection to my husband, David Dunlap, and our son, Will Dunlap, for so much, in so many ways. And for their belief in this wily adventure from the start—even when my nerve failed me.

About the Author

Marianne Boruch's eleven books of poetry include *Bestiary Dark; The Anti-Grief; Eventually One Dreams the Real Thing; Cadaver, Speak; The Book of Hours* (all from Copper Canyon Press); and earlier collections from Oberlin College Press and Wesleyan University Press. Her prose includes a previous memoir, *The Glimpse Traveler* (Indiana University Press), and four books of essays on poetry (Northwestern University, the University of Michigan's Poetry on Poetry series, and Trinity University). Her work has appeared in *The New York Review of Books, Poetry, The New Yorker, The American Poetry Review, New England Review,* the *London Review of Books, The Yale Review,* and other journals. Her watercolors and drawings have appeared in *The Iowa Review,* the *Flannery O'Connor Review, Sycamore Review,* and *Poetry.* Among her honors are the Kingsley Tufts Poetry Award for *The Book of Hours,* Pushcart Prizes, inclusions in *The Best American Poetry,* fellowships from the John Simon Guggenheim Memorial Foundation and the National Endowment for the Arts, and residencies at the Rockefeller Foundation's Bellagio Center, the Anderson Center (Red Wing, Minnesota), Yaddo, and MacDowell. She was a Fulbright Scholar at the University of Edinburgh in 2012 and a Senior Fulbright Research Scholar at the University of Canberra, Australia, in 2019, which inspired her most recent book of poems on that country's astonishing wildlife. Twice she's been a visiting artist at the American Academy in Rome and was named an artist-in-residence at two national parks, Denali and Isle Royale. In 2024, she was an artist-in-residence at the Institute for Advanced Study at Central European University in Budapest. In May 2018, she went rogue and emeritus after thirty-two years of teaching at Purdue University, where she established and directed the MFA program in creative writing. Boruch remains on the faculty at the low-residency graduate program for writers at Warren Wilson College, where she's taught since 1988. She and her husband live in West Lafayette, Indiana, where they raised their son. She continues her decades-long hopeless effort at learning birdsong, which is to say: *who* in the world is saying all that *what* out there.

Also by Marianne Boruch

Poetry
Bestiary Dark
The Anti-Grief
Eventually One Dreams the Real Thing
Cadaver, Speak
The Book of Hours
Grace, Fallen From
Ghost and Oar (chapbook)
Poems: New & Selected
A Stick That Breaks and Breaks
Moss Burning
Descendant
View from the Gazebo

Prose on Poetry
Sing by the Burying Ground: Essays
The Little Death of Self: Nine Essays toward Poetry
In the Blue Pharmacy: Essays on Poetry and Other Transformations
Poetry's Old Air

Memoir
The Glimpse Traveler

Poetry is vital to language and living. Since 1972, Copper Canyon Press has published extraordinary poetry from around the world to engage the imaginations and intellects of readers, writers, booksellers, librarians, teachers, students, and donors.

WE ARE GRATEFUL FOR THE MAJOR SUPPORT PROVIDED BY:

academy of
american poets

OFFICE OF ARTS & CULTURE
SEATTLE

ARTSFUND

THE PAUL G. ALLEN
FAMILY FOUNDATION

Hawthornden
Foundation

POETRY
FOUNDATION

INGRAM
CONTENT GROUP

the point
envision·enact·evolve

McSWEENEY'S

WASHINGTON STATE
ARTS COMMISSION

ART WORKS.

National
Endowment
for the Arts
arts.gov

The Witter Bynner Foundation
for Poetry

TO LEARN MORE ABOUT UNDERWRITING
COPPER CANYON PRESS TITLES,
PLEASE CALL 360-385-4925 EXT. 105

WE ARE GRATEFUL FOR THE MAJOR SUPPORT PROVIDED BY:

Anonymous

Jill Baker and Jeffrey Bishop

Anne and Geoffrey Barker

Donna Bellew

Will Blythe

John Branch

Diana Broze

John R. Cahill

Sarah J. Cavanaugh

Keith Cowan and Linda Walsh

Peter Currie

The Evans Family

Mimi Gardner Gates

Gull Industries Inc.
on behalf of William True

Carolyn and Robert Hedin

David and Jane Hibbard

Bruce S. Kahn

Phil Kovacevich and Eric Wechsler

Maureen Lee and Mark Busto

Ellie Mathews and Carl Youngmann
as The North Press

Larry Mawby and Lois Bahle

Petunia Charitable Fund and
adviser Elizabeth Hebert

Suzanne Rapp and Mark Hamilton

Adam and Lynn Rauch

Emily and Dan Raymond

Joseph C. Roberts

Cynthia Sears

Kim and Jeff Seely

Tree Swenson

Julia Sze

Barbara and Charles Wright

In honor of C.D. Wright
from Forrest Gander

Caleb Young as C. Young Creative

The dedicated interns and faithful
volunteers of Copper Canyon Press

The pressmark for Copper Canyon Press
suggests entrance, connection, and interaction
while holding at its center
an attentive, dynamic space for poetry.

This book is set in Garamond Premier Pro.
Book design by Gopa & Ted2, Inc.
Printed in Canada on archival-quality paper.